Rick

All the Best

University
of Michigan
Business
School Management Series

INNOVATIVE SOLUTIONS TO THE
PRESSING PROBLEMS OF BUSINESS

The mission of the University of Michigan Business School Management Series is to provide accessible, practical, and cutting-edge solutions to the most critical challenges facing businesspeople today. The UMBS Management Series provides concepts and tools for people who seek to make a significant difference in their organizations. Drawing on the research and experience of faculty at the University of Michigan Business School, the books are written to stretch thinking while providing practical, focused, and innovative solutions to the pressing problems of business.

Also available in the UMBS series:

Becoming a Better Value Creator, by Anjan V. Thakor

Achieving Success Through Social Capital, by Wayne Baker

Improving Customer Satisfaction, Loyalty, and Profit,
by Michael D. Johnson and Anders Gustafsson

Strategic Interviewing, by Richaurd Camp, Mary Vielhaber,
and Jack L. Simonetti

Creating the Multicultural Organization, by Taylor Cox

Getting Results, by Clinton O. Longenecker and Jack L. Simonetti

For additional information on any of these titles or future titles
in the series, visit www.umbsbooks.com

Executive Summary

This book introduces a new way to think about compensation in terms of what employees want and need: *cafeteria compensation*. Like cafeteria benefits, it is a response to the need for employee flexibility and choice, values that are growing daily as the workforce becomes more diverse. It is also a response to deep problems in the traditional payroll system—what the author calls *old pay*—and to the changing needs of today's workforce.

Part 1 introduces the total compensation approach. Chapter One sets the stage by examining the problems of old pay and the changing needs and demands of workers in detail. Chapter Two provides an overview of an integrated solution to these problems that adapts two of the core features of cafeteria benefits—flexibility and choice—to the full range of compensation elements. This integrated approach brings together in one place ten key variables, from base pay to the *"X" factor*—a personal element desired by an individual employee. Accounting for all these aspects of reward in one place has a number of advantages for employers and employees alike, but much can be gained by smaller-scale compensation changes that are in line with the overall philosophy recommended here.

The chapters in Part 2 provide a close-up look at each of the ten aspects of compensation, examining problems and solutions specific to each. Chapter Three considers *base pay*, or salary. Chapter Four examines *augmented pay*, that is, one-time payments from overtime to stock options. Chapter Five looks at *indirect pay*, or benefits. Chapter Six surveys issues connected with *works-pay*— the employer-provided resources that employees would otherwise have to purchase to do their jobs, from uniforms to cell phones to office equipment—and *perks-pay*, the perquisites that leverage employers' ability to enhance employees' compensation. Chapter Seven examines *opportunity for advancement* and *opportunity for growth*. Employees have traditionally been vitally interested in the former; increasingly, as firms become flatter and opportunity for advancement up the ladder dwindles, their interest is transferring to the latter. Opportunity for growth includes all the chances the firm provides to learn and grow on the job, whether through onsite training and education or offsite programs and tuition support.

Chapter Eight examines three variables from the "softer side" of compensation. *Psychic income* addresses the emotional satisfaction that workers derive from both the work and the workplace. *Quality of life* addresses the issue, Can you have a work life and the rest of your life, too? Finally, the *X factor* represents employees' individual wants and needs that employers may be able to satisfy with a bit of imagination—and that can make all the difference to attracting and keeping high-quality people.

If rethinking compensation in terms of these ten variables sounds ambitious, it is—but it is not orders-of-magnitude more ambitious than the transition many companies have already made to cafeteria benefits. Part 3 consists of one chapter that considers the issues involved in both small-scale and large-scale organizational change. It devotes special attention to the challenge of changing a compensation system and determining whether to attack compensation issues in small steps or in one large leap.

The Compensation Solution

How to Develop
an Employee-Driven
Rewards System

John E. Tropman

 JOSSEY-BASS
A Wiley Company
San Francisco

Published by

JOSSEY-BASS
A Wiley Company
350 Sansome St.
San Francisco, CA 94104

www.josseybass.com

Jossey-Bass books and products are available through most bookstores. To contact
Jossey-Bass directly, call (888) 378-2537, fax to (800) 605-2665, or visit our website
at www.josseybass.com.

Substantial discounts on bulk quantities of Jossey-Bass books are available to corporations, professional associations, and other organizations. For details and discount information, contact the special sales department at Jossey-Bass.

We at Jossey-Bass strive to use the most environmentally sensitive paper stocks available to us. Our publications are printed on acid-free recycled stock whenever possible,
and our paper always meets or exceeds minimum GPO and EPA requirements.

Credits appear on p. 261.

Library of Congress Cataloging-in-Publication Data

Tropman, John E.
    The compensation solution: how to develop an employee-driven
rewards system/John E. Tropman.
        p. cm.—(University of Michigan Business School
management series)
Includes index.
    ISBN 0-7879-5401-2
    1. Compensation management—United States.   2. Employee fringe
benefits—United States.   I. Title: How to develop an
employee-driven rewards system.   II. Title.   III. Series.
    HF5549.5.C67 T76   2001
    658.3'22—dc21

2001001166

FIRST EDITION
HB Printing   10 9 8 7 6 5 4 3 2 1

Contents

Series Foreword

Welcome to the University of Michigan Business School Management Series. The books in this series address the most urgent problems facing business today. The series is part of a larger initiative at the University of Michigan Business School (UMBS) that ties together a range of efforts to create and share knowledge through conferences, survey research, interactive and distance training, print publications, and new media.

It is just this type of broad-based initiative that sparked my love affair with UMBS in 1984. From the day I arrived I was enamored with the quality of the research, the quality of the MBA program, and the quality of the Executive Education Center. Here was a business school committed to new lines of research, new ways of teaching, and the practical application of ideas. It was a place where innovative thinking could result in tangible outcomes.

The UMBS Management Series is one very important outcome, and it has an interesting history. It turns out that every year five thousand participants in our executive program fill out a marketing survey in which they write statements indicating the most important problems they face. One day Lucy Chin, one of our administrators, handed me a document containing all these statements. A content analysis of the data resulted in a list of forty-five pressing problems. The topics ranged from growing a company to managing personal stress. The list covered a wide territory, and I started to see its potential. People in organizations tend to be driven by a very traditional set of problems, but the solutions evolve. I went to my friends at Jossey-Bass to discuss a publishing project. The discussion eventually grew into the University of Michigan Business School Management Series—Innovative Solutions to the Pressing Problems of Business.

The books are independent of each other, but collectively they create a comprehensive set of management tools that cut across all the functional areas of business—from strategy to human resources to finance, accounting, and operations. They draw on the interdisciplinary research of the Michigan faculty. Yet each book is written so a serious manager can read it quickly and act immediately. I think you will find that they are books that will make a significant difference to you and your organization.

Robert E. Quinn, Consulting Editor
M.E. Tracy Distinguished Professor
University of Michigan Business School

Foreword

The first two decades of the twenty-first century will experience a continuing shortage of qualified employees. Even with the most conservative of economic forecasts, the demographics of our workforce speak loudly: recruiting will be even tougher than in the past decade.

The human resources headlines focus on "the war for talent." But the real war is for organizational success in the marketplace, and it will be fought by the people we have. Most human resources operations have a strategy for recruiting. They expect it to be more expensive, and they are willing to plow more money into it. It has become a bidding war, with stock options, signing bonuses, perks, special developmental assignments, and, perhaps most important, an environment that promises an opportunity to succeed.

Few human resources operations, however, have a strategy for retention—that is, for productive retention. It is a good deal less expensive to keep people than to get new ones. Plus the new ones do not have a valuable commodity—the unique knowledge of how the organization works.

John Tropman's total compensation solution offers human resource and compensation professionals a new way of thinking about how to retain a productive workforce. We continue to rely on being competitive in the labor market as our primary retention strategy, but that is just table stakes. We have to try new approaches, ones that often seem pretty far out. As John points out, however, "pretty far out," "impractical," and "an administrative nightmare" were applied twenty years ago to the idea of expanding group incentive plans to all employees to provide a common focus on the critical success factors of the organization. The same was said about involving workforces in improving performance rather than just relying on management making the decisions and employees carrying them out. John's best example is that of flexible benefits, once radical and now the norm.

The total compensation approach that John advocates is actually one solution of many. It may begin with a selected group of employees rather than an entire workforce. Human resource professionals are a conservative group, for good reason and as a result of hard lessons learned. (Remember Behavioral Anchored Rating Scales and broad-based skill-based pay?) But John's next steps are based on a compelling logic: employees are more important to our success than ever before; they will continue to be scarce; they continue to be more independent; they have less loyalty to the organization and more to their profession; they relish personalized treatment. John's work provides some very creative ideas on how to use these realities to everyone's advantage.

The Compensation Solution is a challenging work and well worth the decade it has taken to develop. We owe it a close examination out of consideration for both our employees and our organizations.

Jerry L. McAdams
Former national practice leader,
rewards and recognition
Watson Wyatt Worldwide

Preface

Several years ago, the editor of the University of Michigan Business School Management Series, Bob Quinn, asked me to consider teaching a new course. It was called "Reward Systems." As chair of the Organizational Behavior and Human Resources Management group at the Business School, Bob was interested in something a bit more current than the old "comp and benefits" course. His vision was a broader one, and he deserves recognition and appreciation for seeing—quite awhile ago—the directions firms would need to take.

I came to the task as an organizational sociologist with an interest in organizational design and organizational policy, especially those aspects of firm policy that—like benefits—served larger social ends as well. I did not have a traditional comp and benefits background, and the idea of a Reward Systems course made perfect sense to me. I should have known; if something makes perfect sense to me it is usually a bad sign. My excitement came from the idea that one ought to be able to tie the energy of thought—which I was talking about in my book *Managing Ideas in the Creating Organization* (Quorum, 1998)—to a framework of intrinsic and extrinsic rewards that created appreciation and motivation for workers and management alike. Right! It turned out, of course, that managers and firms talked rewards, but they paid salaries.

I began by interviewing lots of MBA students about what they wanted from their workplace. I then interviewed other professional students in law, medicine, social work, and other fields in Ann Arbor and elsewhere. Through my work with for-profit firms, nonprofit agencies, and government bureaus, I had access to a significant number of employees as well. In a series of focus groups I explored with them what kinds of rewards they wanted from their workplace, and what trade-offs they were making. I asked them what they thought about a range of value dilemmas that bedevil pay systems, like fair play versus fair share, security versus risk, rewarding results versus rewarding effort, and lifetime employment versus earning your right to a job. I asked them what a *raise* was and why they got it (they were, mostly, unsure), why they were actually paid (also unsure), and how they defined ideas like *equity* and *equality* (also unsure!). I asked them what upset them about their compensation, and a host of other questions as well.

The results were, in a word, rewarding. For one thing, it was from that research that I developed the ten-variable compensation equation used in this book. I found that almost everyone wanted the same things. That is a major finding upon which this work is based. What people did not agree on, however, was how much of them they wanted at any given time. Hence, a second major finding was that they wanted to *choose* the way their compensation package came together—at least to a degree.

Initially I resisted this outlandish idea. After all, even if I was not a comp and benefits guy, I did know that pay was, well, pay. One size fit all. Or did it? The more I thought about their answers, the more I thought they had the right answer and I had the wrong one. They were thinking out of the box, and I was in the box. One MBA student said, "Hell, it's just customization. I customize my car to get what I want; I can choose from umpteen brands of toothpaste at the store; I should be able to have something to say about my compensation vehicles." And he was right.

Some other pieces of information were filling in as well. My MBA class was very diverse—about 40 percent were women, up sharply from years before. And the students came from all over the world. The age span was wide, from younger twenty-somethings to older fifty-somethings. There were straights and gays, singles and students with five kids, not a few who were caring for older relatives, and so on. The lifestyle range was quite wide. And I did not have to look at my classes for this insight; every workplace demographic study was saying the same thing. So it was very clear that, if one size had ever fit all, that day was over. Employees had a range of needs; those needs had to be addressed by (to borrow some phrases from Tom Peters) a nimble, fleet-of-foot compensation program.

My interviewees had similar categories of needs, but different arrays of them (for different individuals in the group at the same time, as well as for the same individuals over time). What they did *not* know was why they were actually paid, or why they were given raises. In fact, they did not understand very much about the compensation system at all. This finding taught me that compensation communication is a separate and important element of compensation policy.

I also interviewed employers and specialists in comp and benefits. It turned out that there was no central place in most firms where all compensation-related issues could roost. Indeed, there were competition and conflict between and among elements of the compensation system. While employees were struggling to craft a system that made sense to them, employers were striving to keep "each tub on its own bottom." This finding was discouraging to me. It is going to take more work than I thought to coordinate and articulate compensation elements. Even though, in the immortal words of Henry Mintzberg, "fit is it," compensation systems are still fragmented and poorly rationalized. We are still, in Steve Kerr's phrase, pursuing the "folly of rewarding A while hoping for B." My hope is that this book can provide a new perspective—built, to be sure, on some things that are already under way—that points the way to the total compensation solution of the future.

■ Acknowledgments

When Lance Armstrong writes about bicycle racing, he tell us how much of a group effort victory really is. Groups of riders circle round the leader and protect him or her from wind, other riders, and hazards, allowing maximum use of the rider's energy.[1] I think books are like that. My name is on the cover, but I am surrounded by others who made that possible.

Bob Quinn, master author and speaker and my colleague at the Michigan Business School, was the man who first invited me to teach a different kind of "comp and benefits" course and initiated this series of books from the University of Michigan. He deserves thanks. Other colleagues, including Wayne Baker, Paula Caproni, Jeff De Graff, and others contributed, through conversations and suggestions, to a "yeasty" intellectual environment at Michigan.

The Jossey-Bass crew—especially Byron Schneider and Cedric Crocker—were always supportive. John Bergez scrutinized the text with a wary eye and improved every portion. Sheri Gilbert and Carolyn Uno performed vital checks on the manuscript in a consummately professional manner.

Then there are the "research subjects," as it were—the students in my rewards class and other classes, as well as the employers and workers with whom I have talked about these concepts and whose interests, wishes, and suggestions about what a really "knock your socks off" compensation system would look like helped me in every way.

Compensation professionals—Don Lowman from Towers Perrin, Norman Harberger from Harberger Associates, Lindsay Gross from Rock Financial, Joan Schnider from Zingerman's, Eileen Vernor from Borders—have been helpful beyond measure.

The professional always depends on the personal, though, and I want to thank my wife Penny with a special mention. She has a business of her own, and struggles with issues of rewards on a daily basis. And as I talk about workplace issues with my children, I get the recipient's eye view of what universities, libraries, and the military could do to make their lives easier, their work more appreciated and meaningful, and their energy "zapped" instead of "sapped."[2]

So to that large group of riders who have bunched up with me and helped me, thank you, each and every one.

February 2001   John E. Tropman
Glen Arbor, Michigan

The
Compensation
Solution

PART 1

The Total Compensation Solution

P ay is one of the most important elements of the modern firm. It is what *compensates, drives, motivates,* and *rewards* employees for the work they do. Or it does the opposite of these things.

Old pay—my term for most past and many current pay structures—winds up being a frozen system based on tenure, entitlement, and internal equity. "New pay" began to articulate a more cogent direction for pay systems, linking pay to the success of the employee and the firm. "*New* new pay," or the concept introduced here, proposes a comprehensive system of ten variables that together form the total compensation solution. A key element of this approach is that it involves a degree of customization and choice: *cafeteria compensation,* to go with the cafeteria benefits programs that have already proved so successful.

Chapter One discusses the problems with old pay in some detail and outlines the elements of the total compensation solution. Chapter Two zeroes in on the ten variables of total compensation and addresses how they can be linked to create a comprehensive solution to the challenge of compensation. Even if firms elect to move in the direction of total compensation in small steps rather than one big leap, it is crucial to have a clear vision of the ultimate destination—one that suits the firms and employees of today and tomorrow.

From Old Pay to Total Compensation

This book is about a total compensation solution, or what used to be called *pay and benefits*. The total compensation solution is based on a rethinking of employee compensation and investment systems into an employee-driven system I call *cafeteria compensation*. It is the *new* "new pay."

Compensation thinkers have been raising questions about the structure of existing (and often rigid) pay systems for some time. In 1971, Ed Lawler—way ahead of his time—introduced the then-shocking idea of linking pay and organizational development, in a book of that title.[1] W. Edwards Deming pointed to the random nature of the relationship between pay and performance in *Out of the Crisis* (1982).[2] Lawler scored again in 1990 with his classic *Strategic Pay: Aligning Organizational Strategies and Pay Systems.*[3] And in 1992, Jay Schuster and Patricia Zingheim introduced the concept of *new pay* in another book (with a foreword by—you guessed it—Ed Lawler!).[4]

Recently some new books have continued the contribution of these thinkers. In 2000, Lawler talked about rewards in *Rewarding Excellence,*[5] and Zingheim and Schuster reversed the order of their names but not their message in *Pay Them Right!*[6] Notice, though, that most of these books and thinkers, and many others, are still talking about *pay.* We Americans have pay on the brain. But is pay all there is? The answer is *no.* It is no because pay is often badly configured and no because other things besides pay are needed to attract, retain, and motivate employees.

I think Jerry McAdams puts it best in his terrific book, *The Reward Plan Advantage.*[7] He sees rewards and "the reward plan" as a way to energize the people you have and hone their skills and attention so that they are operating at close to peak performance. As any orchestra conductor or coach knows, just having the people, even talented people (or, perhaps, *especially* talented people) does not a good performance make. I use these examples because Jerry also speaks out in favor of team-based rewards. In our individualistic, each-tub-on-its-own-bottom society, this is courageous as well as correct. Others have talked about the importance of systems—W. Edwards Deming was one. But Jerry gives us some clues about how to approach actually doing it.

He does something else I would like to endorse, as well. He talks about *best principles* rather than best practices. This book is like that; it presents a set of principles to stimulate locally developed practices. Jerry comments, "There are few, if any, 'best practices.' Improving performance through people demands that you create plans unique to your organization. There is danger in cookie cutter answers."[8] You can say that again. And his words apply very well here. Take the cafeteria compensation idea and, with the help of your employees—the very ones who are the intended recipients of the plan—use it to build a package for your shop that makes sense for your shop. *That* will be something that works.

Let me add one more word about employee involvement. Throughout this book I will be suggesting that you ask employees what they think and want. It seems so obvious. But many of the problems with the current system stem, in part, from the absence of this simple step. Remember that involvement is as American as apple pie. The Boston Tea Party was about the absence of just that—"No taxation without representation." American businesses have fallen into the same mistake the British government did, but we can learn from their mistakes.

■ Cafeteria Compensation: Building in Diversity and Choice

The idea of cafeteria compensation goes beyond pay alone to propose a rewards and investment *system*—a group of ten variables that together encompass the variety of kinds of compensation that today's employees want from work. Pay is among them, of course (including both base pay, or salary, and one-time pay received in the form of overtime or bonuses). But in addition to monetary rewards, contemporary employees want and are increasingly demanding reward *diversity* and reward *choice.* In today's diverse, global economy one size does not fit all. Employers are finding that employees want a range of different things from the workplace. Employees will even exchange some level of base pay to get some of the other things they want, such as the psychic income derived from a job that an employee considers meaningful or, as one woman told me, a "jerk-free environment." Moreover, not only do different employees have different needs at a given time but the needs of individual employees change over time.

This roiling of the waters of need creates a pressure for choice. Choice is everywhere today, in the workplace no less than in the supermarket. Employees are increasingly looking at their paycheck the way they look at their market basket—they want some say in what goes into it. They want the chance to configure, within reasonable limits, their own rewards systems.

The model for the system proposed here is the cafeteria benefits plans that allow employees to tailor their benefits to their own needs and interests and those of their families. In a similar fashion, cafeteria compensation increases the quality and diversity of the rewards available as well as the level of employee choice. This system is one that can attract, motivate, and retain employees because, like a fine restaurant, it offers quality, variety, and choice. Because it goes beyond pay, even the "new pay" to be discussed further on, I have called it the *new* new pay.

Why do we need such a dramatic transformation of compensation systems? There are two basic reasons. One is that there is lots wrong with "old pay" for all workers. The second is that newer workers, in particular, need a different compensation mix from the one that suited their predecessors. This chapter examines these fundamental issues with old pay in some detail and then sketches the outline of the total compensation solution. Chapter Two presents the elements of the solution in greater detail.

■ Before You Start

The remainder of this chapter deals with some of the problems with old pay, and then discusses some of the reasons those problems persist. The focus here is on the private sector. (The public and nonprofit sectors are briefly discussed in the Appendix, but the discussion in this chapter can also be applied to them fairly directly. Their picture is much the same in terms of problems, though played out in terms of smaller dollar amounts.)

Many readers will find the list of problems familiar, and perhaps discouraging. Further, discouragement about their persistence—a feeling perhaps that we are trapped in the current system and there is nothing we can do—may be the main thing that comes to mind. The very fact of the problems' familiarity means we need to face them squarely.

There are several points I urge you to keep in mind. First, it is important to lay the problems out as a first step to any process of improvement. Compensation is the "elephant in the living room" of most organizations—large, oppressive, and unaddressed. Attention to pay systems is often nonattention. It falls into what Harvard's Chris Argyris called "defensive routines"—they are not discussible, and their nondiscussibility is not discussible!

Second, cafeteria compensation provides a solution to some of the pressing problems of compensation. At one level it can be a solution-map. It provides a vision of where we should go, even if progress is slow. That is, it provides a systematic way of thinking about compensation issues. More concretely, it is a system that can actually be implemented. At this level, some people may balk. One can imagine the comments. *"Letting individuals construct some of their own pay package? Can't do it! Could never do it! Must have been designed by a professor!"* However, remember that we have already been through this kind of change when we went from one-size-fits-all defined benefits packages to cafeteria benefits. Many of the same cautionary tales were told, the same hand-wringing went on, but, voilà! Here we are today with cafeteria plans all over the place, employees picking and choosing, companies crafting overall models to the needs of their particular firm, and so on. We have already made this journey.

I see two basic approaches to change. If you take the vision approach, in which cafeteria compensation is the ultimate goal, then you can embark on *transactional* change—one step at a time, building on small wins toward the final, comprehensive plan. This is an evolutionary approach to change. On the other hand, you might wish to try the whole thing, whether for the entire organization or for a single unit. That would be *transformational* change, or revolution. Each approach has pluses and minuses, as I'll discuss in Chapter Nine. You will need to think of your own setting, energy, and support as you go forward. The point is to be open to what a new and more effective system would look like, and the advantages it would bring, whether or not you can picture getting there all at once.

■ The Many Failures of Old Pay

In the typical old pay approach, compensation can be thought of as consisting of five parts:

- Base pay
- Annual merit raise
- Benefits
- A few perks
- Occasional gratuities (Christmas bonus, and so on)

This way of thinking about compensation poses a number of problems from both the organization's point of view and that of the employee. I will discuss them in more detail throughout the book, but it helps to get an overview of some of the most general and pressing problems. Here I'll mention nine of them. The first four are inherent in old pay itself. The remaining five concerns are more generalized problems of old pay *systems*.

Inherent Problems with Old Pay

Some problems are inherent in the way old pay is conceptualized:

- *Pay becomes entitlement driven.* In old pay, employees feel they are entitled to their pay, and to raises in pay, unconnected with any accomplishments they produce.
- *Increases cap out.* With old pay, increases are cut off when the employee reaches the top of a job's range. Employers thus "bump" workers to higher job classifications solely to give them more pay.
- *Failure to motivate.* Old pay does not motivate because it is mostly unlinked to the employee's production and contribution. To begin with, base pay (before "merit" adjustments) is frequently unconnected to any results or accomplishments. It is almost as if one is paid a salary just to show up.
- *Annuitized.* With old pay, each raise goes into the base. Hence employers pay year in and year out for last year's accomplishments. This means that employee investments keep costing more without any parallel increase in productivity. It is like throwing good money after bad.

Problems with Old Pay Systems

Employers often realize that old pay creates entitlement, cap-out, motivational, and annuitization problems. But like runners with stones in their shoes, they can't seem to find time to stop and change the situation. However, the story does not end there. Old pay systems drive some more general problems for employers that compound the initial set. Compensation systems are supposed to attract, retain, and motivate employees. Most pay systems fail on this larger count. Many current pay systems give the wrong message. Their very structure communicates messages that are at variance with the publicly expressed wishes and commitments of executives and the corporation. The system itself fails to walk the talk. It is hard to attract and retain when the gap between pronouncement and practice is large. More specifically,

- *Thinking about compensation is fragmented.* In most organizations many different types of people think about the various forms of compensation. Some think about pay, others think about benefits, others think about training, still others think about employee discounts. Some think about "rewards"; others think about "investments." No one thinks about the whole package.
- *Employee cost calculations are limited and hidden.* Because the thinking about employee rewards and investments, as well as their administration, is distributed throughout the firm, the company has very limited ability to ascertain the total cost of an employee to the organization. Correlatively, it has a limited sense of what the total employee cost *should* be and a limited sense of the replacement cost for that employee.
- *Failure to leverage the system.* The fact that so many people are involved in "rewards" means that firms cannot leverage the system by aligning all rewards in a single package.
- *Lack of employee involvement.* The lack of involvement on the part of employees is a characteristic of old pay systems. In spite of the cultural history of America, which is built on participation of those involved ("No Taxation without Representation!"), many firms simply tell employees what their compensation is—they wouldn't think of asking what people want.
- *Failure to drive change.* A failure to drive change retards change. As the old community organizers would put it, "If you are not part of the solution, you are part of the problem." Old pay tends to keep organizations from recalibrating rewards systems and aligning them to new goals and strategies. Em-

ployees work in teams, for example, but are paid as individuals. Hello!

Benefits represent another type of problem. They have become a large cost, 30 percent and up of salaries and wages. But employers get little benefit from benefits. Indeed, they are trapped in the hammerlock of "defined benefit" mind-sets, both for medical and pension elements. Having promised a certain level of medical coverage, for example, they are caught in the trap of having to provide that coverage regardless of cost. The same is true of pensions. Defined benefit plans trap the employer with high expectations and unfunded or underfunded liabilities.

As for perks, except at the executive level, they are being phased out (except for discounts on company products) because they have become taxable and require lots of record keeping. Also, employees frequently are unclear about who is entitled to what. Finally, the occasional gratuities that firms throw to employees have little motivational value, as they are neither *prewards* (rewards in anticipation of accomplishment) nor *postwards* (rewards that follow accomplishment); connectivity and line of sight are lost.

These and other problems of old pay create an organizational subsystem that is always lagging behind the other parts of the organization. No wonder Steve Kerr talks about the "folly of rewarding A while hoping for B."[9]

Problems from the employer's side of course have impacts on employees as well, though the employee perspective is usually different. Employees are mostly satisfied with their pay, but very dissatisfied with the pay system. The "capping out" problem traps them in some rank; the raises are usually small (because they are across the board). Money comes, or does not, independent of accomplishments, and this apparent randomness is a huge demotivator. Oddly, the system we think should attract and retain often dissuades and dismisses.

One Professional's View of the Problems with Old Pay

I'm not alone in pointing out the deficiencies of the standard pay system; other practicing consultants concur. When I talked with Don Lowman (a principal of Towers Perrin) about compensation-related issues, he stressed the following five issues with old pay:

1. *Structurally behind the times.* Organizations have changed their structures a lot in recent years. They have become flatter—with fewer layers—and they have revised career paths. Job responsibilities are more flexible and more ambiguous. And there have been fundamental shifts in workforce profile and expectations. Meanwhile, new sources of competition are continually emerging.

Despite these changes, many organizations persist in using outmoded elements of pay programs: narrow and confining salary ranges (although this feature diminished greatly in the late 1990s); salary programs that continue to reward heavily for traditional values (for example, scope of responsibility and number of direct reports) rather than current needs (competencies and hot skills); job-based criteria for determining pay opportunities; use of market pay data from traditional competitors; overreliance on cash for retention and motivation; and merit pay processes that provide little opportunity to recognize differences in individual contributions.

2. *Culturally behind the times.* Current pay systems are based on an implicit contract with employees that expired without being renewed. The old contract said, "If you work hard, the firm will take care of you." Taking care of you meant, largely, that you would keep your job, almost no matter what you did (or, more likely, did not do), and that all employees were entitled to some market adjustment to stay "whole." Pay, in the old contract, involved the following elements:

- *Cost of living increase.* This increase came every year.
- *Increases attached to base.* That is, raises were added to the employee's base pay.

- *Increases largely based on seniority.* Raises were greater for those who had been with the organization longer, sometimes because length of service was directly figured in, and sometimes because, using a percentage increase model, those who had been there longer made more money and hence received a bigger dollar increase.
- *Grade-based promotion.* Promotion to higher salary grades (based on seniority) carried employees to higher pay potential, both in salary and bonus. (Bonuses were typically calibrated as a percent of salary so in this model the more you made the more you got.)
- *Trophies.* At various anniversary dates of employment (five years, ten years, and so on) employees were given mementos of their association with the company: the hat, the pen and pencil set, the watch. Usually the watch was given (as it was to my grandfather) on retirement, just when the employee didn't need it. Trophies would, of course, have been more meaningful if they had been given in relationship to some actual accomplishment rather than just for hanging around.
- *Holiday gifts.* At holiday times, especially Christmas, the company gave employees a gift—a turkey, a ham, a basket of fruit.
- *Bonuses.* Periodically, but often unconnected or connected only hazily to anything the employee could figure out, a bonus was provided.

This old contract was based on old rules, which in turn were driven by the old organization. It has run smack into a new culture, fueled in part by new organizations, new generations of workers (Gen X), by new consciousness in workers who are fed up with being treated as second-class citizens (older workers and women of all ages), and by traditional workers who are sick of being evaluated on the basis of *facetime* (time in the plant). As many firms are beginning to realize, this new culture calls for a new work contract.

The new contract says, "If we outperform the market, you will share the rewards." This approach is more of a "contingent contract." It sets goals of production and invites employees, units, and divisions to share in them. Perhaps the most famous statement of this kind of approach was articulated by General Electric's Jack Welch. Each division at GE was to be number one or number two in its market. Otherwise one of three things would happen: "fix, close, or sell." If a division maintained its desired position, however, workers in that division were entitled to share in the profits.

The new contract has several elements that are quite different from the old one:

- *Employees have to earn the right to competitive pay.* No more entitlement. No one is guaranteed anything, necessarily. Personal pay is driven primarily by performance, which takes into account not only individual contributions but also group and company performance.
- *Self-funded at the unit level.* As in the GE approach, the profit is shared by profit centers within the organization. Employees may have several sources of pay, and what they get depends on the performance of the various units.
- *Variable pay.* At the individual level, pay (or salary) becomes somewhat variable. Employees are not entitled to their entire pay unless they meet certain benchmarks; however, if they exceed the benchmarks, they can make more than their agreed-upon base.
- *Line of sight.* Most organizations have tried to adopt approaches with a stronger line of sight between the pay individuals receive and the performance results they most directly influence. As a result, many variable-pay arrangements are tied to business-unit results.

- *Unit gainsharing.* The bonus pool is figured on the gain the unit makes above market averages, minus costs and scrap.
- *Firm gainsharing.* This portion of the bonus comes from the overall firm performance, again, looking at the amount above market.
- *Market adjustment to base.* Base pay is adjusted, overall and for individuals, depending on market forces, not seemingly random acts of the Human Resources Department.

New-contract thinking is part of—indeed the basis of and driver for—the total compensation solution explored in this book.

3. *Strategically out of whack.* A third problem identified by Lowman is that traditional pay systems are misaligned (or unaligned) with fundamental business strategies. For example, the firm states that part of its strategy is to be a top performer. Yet the same company targets median competitive pay levels and rewards only senior executives for financial performance. What the strategy calls for is increasing target pay opportunities, creating incentive leverage, and rewarding everyone for contributions to financial performance.

Here's another example. The company states a strategic goal of increasing long-term value for shareholders, yet it ties bonuses exclusively to short-term financial performance. What it needs to do is to identify performance measures linked to shareholder value creation and incorporate these into incentive programs.

Or consider an announced strategy of achieving competitive advantage through people. The same company may manage pay programs to minimize cost, equate employees with cost, and cling to the belief that employees should not be paid too much (the sticker shock hypothesis). Aligning pay systems with the strategic goal requires managing pay programs to maximize returns. It means treating employees as the ratio of output and cost, and rethinking sticker shock by paying less attention to whether pay exceeds some competitive norm and more attention to whether the firm is getting its money's worth through performance accomplishments.

4. *Significant say/do gaps.* Old pay systems frequently are in conflict with the values espoused publicly by management. For example, managers may proclaim values like these:

- Link executive and shareholder interests.
- Develop a highly skilled workforce.
- Encourage employee involvement.
- Promote teamwork.
- Recognize outstanding contributions.
- Focus on quality and customer satisfaction.

Meanwhile, the pay system

- Allows frequent churning of stock options.
- Uses traditional job-evaluation approaches.
- Ignores or discounts employees' views in developing pay programs.
- Uses restrictive merit-pay approaches as a primary reward device.
- Ties bonuses to accounting measures of performance.

5. *Top management double standard.* In many organizations, there are only weak links between pay and performance at the very top, at the same time that management insists on stronger links elsewhere. Thus firms pay their top people large bonuses in the face of languishing performance, make "mega" options grants with multimillion-dollar paybacks in the face of below-average returns, and generally eliminate pay risk for top executives. What messages do such practices communicate to the rest of the organization?

"We are exempt from the pay-for-performance doctrine we claim
   for you."
"We should have less financial risk than our shareholders."
"We should make money from company stock even if the own-
   ers lose."
"Entitlement is out—except for us."

Combining my recital of issues with old pay with Don
Lowman's observations (and the similar problems in the public
sector mentioned in the Appendix), I am reminded of the gal-
lows joke—"Other than that, Mrs. Lincoln, how did you enjoy
the play?" Yet even though many compensation specialists,
human resource officers, CEOs, and employees would agree
with these problems—and indeed could add to the list—somehow the band plays on. Why should that be the case?

Structural Lag and Means Ritualism

Social scientists call this kind of situation *structural lag*. Structural lag occurs when a culture and its values have progressed
and the organizational structure has not caught up. It is, in other
terms, what the sociologist Robert Merton called "means ritualism."[10] New ends have come into play, but we are still stuck
using the old methods and cannot seem to get out of them.

Structural lag and means ritualism emerge from two broad
groups of processes. One group involves the lack of a change
strategy; that is, we keep on doing things the same way because
we cannot think of anything new, or we do not have ways to implement the new thing, or we do not have the energy to implement the new thing.

The second group results from an organization's muscle
memory. When organizations (or people) do something one way
for a while, it becomes a *default style*—action taken without

thought. Default styles are tougher to change than more surface behaviors, a fact that makes the lack of a change strategy even more important. Worse, default styles emerge most powerfully under stressful conditions—that is, when organizations (and persons) fall back on the "tried and true." The tried and true, of course, are the very things that got the organization into the stressful condition in the first place, so their employment is usually 100 percent contraindicated.

False Theories About Employees

Default styles continue to pop up despite the repeated failure of the tried and true solutions to address new conditions, however. They are sustained in part by false theories about employees, which form an important element in resistance to change:

- Misunderstanding of the motivational components of performance
- Misunderstanding of the importance of Theory Y
- Misunderstanding of job structure and the order of satisfaction with work and the completion of good work
- Misunderstanding of job satisfiers and job dissatisfiers
- Misunderstanding of the motivational structure of the employee
- Misunderstanding of the cultural conflict between achievement and equality in the workplace
- Misunderstanding of the motivational hierarchy of needs

It's useful to consider the ramifications of these seven misunderstandings.

1. *Components of performance.* Employers typically undervalue their own responsibility for employee performance. Performance results from a complex interaction of ability multiplied by motivation. (I provide a more detailed discussion of perfor-

mance in Chapter Eight.) Employees with lesser ability can compensate with higher motivation; those with great ability do not have to work as hard as others do to achieve even better results.

The manager's job is not only to recruit for ability and motivation but to develop them on the job. Organizations are only now beginning to understand that it is almost impossible to "recruit" to greatness. Recruitment is only a beginning.

Ability and motivation in turn have components. Aptitude, of course, is a factor in ability. But most of us tend to overrate aptitude and diminish the importance of training and resources. These components need to be provided by management, in cooperation with employee input.

Motivation also has components: desire and commitment. Here again, employees have their part to play; the firm, though, has to create followers who want to come to their work and are committed to the importance of it.

The misunderstanding, then, is an almost total reliance on the employee to "produce" performance. It is one of the important elements of cluelessness about the firm's role in becoming a high-performing organization.

2. *Theory Y.* One of the most famous distinctions in management is that between Theory X and Theory Y.[11] Theory X refers to a belief that workers do not want to work and that an employer therefore needs a reward and punishment system (very much like that used in animal training) to assure that workers show up and shape up. Part of Theory X is the notion of "span of control," the idea that the number of workers a supervisor can supervise is about five. Each worker has to be closely watched. And the watchers have to be watched. You can see how this produces a tall pyramid with a narrow base and many levels. Part of the organizational structure that is now passing was driven "by the numbers."

Theory Y argues that that workers want to work and get satisfaction out of doing a good job. The job of the organization is not to control the worker but to provide resources so the worker can get the job done. Theory Y is the one needed for today's flatter, more self-directed organizations. This theory replaces span of control ($n = 5$) with "span of communication." Managers do not check on workers; workers check in with managers when there is a problem.

The problem is that we continue to have a Theory X mindset in a Theory Y environment. Old compensation systems are still, in many ways, driven by Theory X thinking. No wonder they hold back change and diminish the organization's productivity.

3. *Structure of the job.* Many employers believe that satisfied employees produce good work. Hence they try to "improve morale" in the hope of improving quality. The trouble is, they have the causality backwards. What employers should do is improve the structure of the job first. Good jobs lead to satisfied workers, and satisfied workers lead to higher quality and productivity. Employees like jobs that have significance (meaningful work), wholeness (you get to do a complete package, making the whole salad instead of being "lettuce man"), variety (using different skills and having different assignments), autonomy (being able to work "on your own" in a Theory Y way), and responsibility (being accountable). Employers would be better off if they started by modifying the job rather than the worker. Besides, changing the job is a lot easier.

4. *Satisfiers and dissatisfiers.* One of the casualties of Theory X is that employers fail to see three important things about their employees' relationship to the workplace. First, employees have a wide range of satisfactions from work that begin with the work itself and extend into the social elements of the workplace. Second, there are some surprising things about work that workers do not like and that employers leave largely unattended. Third, the "satisfiers" and the "dissatisfiers" are not the same things, meaning that employers have two tasks: create satisfaction *and* remove dissatisfaction.

Table 1.1 depicts how the combination of satisfiers and dissatisfiers characterizes the desirability of the workplace. Optimally, the employer would like to be the workplace of choice—a place so good to work that people struggle to get there. At the other end of the continuum is the workplace from hell. Scott Adams—through his "Dilbert" series—tells us much about that.[12]

With this picture in mind, consider the following list, which spells out some of the things employees like and dislike. It would be good to study this list. Employees like to be able to achieve—in levels or in tasks. The work itself and the feeling of responsibility have just been mentioned. Attachment, the social dimension of the workplace, is important as well. Each of these things—and money is not among them—are things the employer has to manage, create, and assist over and above money in order to draw and retain employees.

Top Satisfiers	Top Dissatisfiers
Achievement	Company policy and management
Recognition	Supervision
Work itself	Relationship with supervisor
Responsibility	Work conditions
Attachment	Relationships with peers
Growth	Relationships with subordinates

Notice that the dissatisfaction list is heavily relationship-based. One thing employees find problematic about their workplace is the

Table 1.1. Effects of Satisfiers and Dissatisfiers on the Desirability of the Workplace

	Dissatisfiers	
Satisfiers	Few	Many
Many	Employer of choice	A great place to work, but it costs you.
Few	Comme çi, comme ça	The job from hell.

other people in it! As a practical matter, this means—based on the employees I have interviewed—that managers really are not doing their job. People are problems because management does not take appropriate action to provide discipline and structure.

5. *Motivational structure: employees' dual nature.* Most employers think of the employee as a single person. So do most employees. As is so often the case, however, reality is more complex. Some years ago Harvard economist Thomas Schelling came up with a two-self model in an article he titled "Egonomics."[13] Schelling pointed out that the two "selves" embody two different preference schedules: money now (cash in hand) and money later (cash put aside for retirement). There is the good-for-me-now self and the good-for-me-later self. These selves conflict along a range of issues. In a way, employers pay both of these selves, via the monthly check for the here-and-now self and the retirement contribution for the then-and-there self.

A little bit later, Richard Thaler and H. M. Shiffrin developed the "planner/doer" model (they referred to it as the far-sighted planner and the myopic doer).[14] Here's a summary of these views of the dual self:

Here-and-Now Self	*Then-and-There Self*
Fun for me	Good for me
Doer	Planner
Money now	Money later

What this insight means for employers is that there are really two compensation targets: the employees' present and future selves. Philosophers can debate how much compensation should be current and how much deferred. As a practical matter, though, giving employees some choice among forms of current income (salary versus bonus versus opportunity for growth, for example), some choice among forms of deferred income (more retirement versus lump sum at year's end versus deferred payment into future years versus more medical benefits), and some choice between money now and money later makes a lot of sense and gives employees options—something over and above the compensation itself. This kind of choice is what the new new pay provides.

6. *Workplace culture in conflict: the achievers versus the egalitarians.* It is one thing to look at the employee as having two selves—two selves whose needs must be balanced in a compensation system. These two selves ramify into a cultural conflict within the firm. To this cultural conflict we can add other firm-level conflicts that revolve around an achievement orientation versus egalitarianism (see Table 1.2).

One manifestation of this conflict is the clash between the individual-worker view and the team-player view. Do we pay persons or teams? Another has to do with the rules for rewards. Is fair play appropriate, or is fair share a better way to go? Should firms pay top dollar to optimize employee recruitment and retention, or should they pay the going market rate? Do they give rewards to those who deserve it or those who need it? Do they promote based on merit or on seniority?

At the extremes, an organization could have an "achievement" culture made up of the orientations in that column in Table 1.2, or it could have an "equality" culture made up of the

Table 1.2. Achievement Versus Egalitarian Cultures

	Achievement Culture	Egalitarian Culture
Firm culture	Market base	Clan base
Self	Here and now	Then and there
Employee/worker	Solo worker	Ensemble or team worker
Rules for reward	Fair play	Fair share
Goals for rewards	Optimizing	Satisficing
Bases of reward	Worthy	Needy
Bases of promotion	Merit	Seniority

Source: Adapted from John E. Tropman, *The Catholic Ethic in American Society* (San Francisco: Jossey-Bass, 1996).

elements in that column. In reality, of course, all organizational cultures are a blend of achievement and equality. It's the tension between winner-take-all and everyone-gets-rewarded, between "each tub on its own bottom" and "a rising tide lifts all boats." A compensation system that permits some employee customization seems to be a pretty good solution to the problem of how to balance these competing orientations.

   7. *The hierarchy of needs.* Not only are employee needs stretched, they are also stacked, as depicted in Abraham Maslow's famous hierarchy of needs (Figure 1.1). As Gareth Morgan says, Maslow's hierarchy is something of a pile of elastic bags, one atop the other.[15] There are two key elements to Maslow's work that affect us here. One is that the needs are a hierarchy—it is hard to address higher-level needs when lower-level ones remain unfulfilled. The second is that the hierarchy gives employers a checklist that can be used to review the total compensation package.

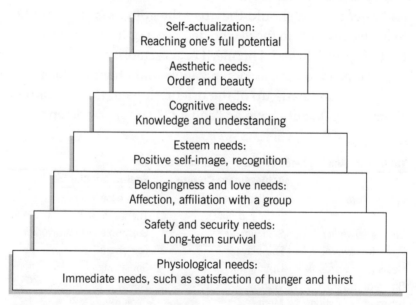

Figure 1.1. **Maslow's Hierarchy of Needs**
Note: In general, lower-order needs must be satisfied before higher-order needs.
Source: Adapted from E. Bruce Goldstein, *Psychology* (Belmont, Calif.: Wadsworth, 1994).

Overall, these seven misunderstandings tend to mean that employers have a rigid, overadministered, and undermanaged compensation system. Things need to change—especially given the composition, needs, and expectations of today's workforce.

■ The New Workforce

The old pay workforce was essentially one of white male bread-winners. Of course, there were working women as well as members of minorities, but they were often relegated to a secondary labor market and certainly paid secondary wages. Their interests did not drive the pay system. The new workforce is far more diverse. Today, women's interests and needs are becoming a serious force in the workplace; it is in part because of unresponsive workplaces that so many women are becoming entrepreneurs. At the same time, individuals from previously minority cultures are achieving dominant numbers in the workplace.

Other aspects of demographics are changing as well. Couples are working. This means, for one thing, that such matters as child care and flextime—quality of life issues—are achieving heightened importance. Then too, families have elders to be concerned about. Firms are offering long-term-care insurance for the parents of workers, as well as health coverage for their children.

Other aspects of family work become key. Workers increasingly think in terms of family income, as opposed to the income of one. Hence employers seeking to attract a worker need to think of what the worker's partner makes as well. A signing bonus of $25,000, for example, an amount most employers would think of as handsome, means little to me if accepting the offer means that my partner loses a $75,000 job. This problem is exacerbated (or as one HR manager put it to me, in a quaintly apt misphrasing, "exasperated") at the upper end because high-income, highly educated men tend to marry high-income, highly educated women. One of the reasons that pay in the traditional sense becomes less important is that any individual's fraction of family income is now reduced.

Further, the idea of what a family is, and what its needs are, becomes more complicated daily. Gay couples, lesbian couples, couples who want to adopt children, and so on each have special needs. All expect to meet some of these needs through the compensation provided by the workplace.

These changes place extraordinary demands on the workplace in general and on the compensation system in particular. American society teaches us that through work—and hence through the workplace—many of our most important needs will be met. Hence the work itself needs to be rewarding—that is, one kind of compensation. We get many of our friends through work; hence, a "jerk-full," toxic organization is unacceptable. Education has also become the province of the firm. As Stan Davis and Jim Botkin discuss in *The Monster Under the Bed,*[16] educational "dominance" has moved from the state to the firm. Employees expect to be educated at the workplace.

Finally, there is the generational perspective. Old pay existed in the era of old values. Those were what Yankelovich called the "giving/getting compact."[17] The giving/getting compact was developed out of the trauma of the Depression of the 1930s and the security of armed forces employment during World War II. It said to employees, you give us loyalty and stay with us, and you'll get security and regular wage increases. You'll also get the security of good fringe benefits (also a product of World War II, when wage and price controls meant that wage increases could not be given). That was the era of Big Blue, U.S. Steel, General Motors, General Electric, and General Mills (an awful lot of "Generals"), when the man in the gray flannel suit (immortalized in the title of Sloan Wilson's popular 1955 book) replaced the man in the army uniform. Old pay is linked to old values systems and subcultures.[18]

Today we have the Boomers, Gen X, and beyond, cohorts with quite different preferences and expectations. Although categorizing people in terms of generations is somewhat hazardous, the following breakdown seems to have some agreement: Veterans, born 1922–1943; Boomers, born 1943–1960; Gen Xers, born 1960–1980; and Nexters, born 1980 to the present. Each generation has a somewhat different schedule of preferences. But as Veterans move out and others move in, proportions change and the workforce changes. Overall, the preference schedule shown in Table 1.3 seems to apply to Gen X and beyond.[19]

It seems clear from the list in Table 1.3 that choice, personal ability to customize work site activities and rewards, authenticity, and independence are among the kinds of compensation that workers from this generation seek from their workplace. To become the employer of choice, firms need to totally rethink their compensation system. Old pay simply will not work.

As early as 1993, the *National Study of the Changing Workforce* came to this conclusion: "Taken together, the responses of

Table 1.3. Turn-Offs and Turn-Ons for Gen X

Turn-Offs	Turn-Ons
High stress work situations	Marketable learning opportunities
Incentive programs that are "here today and gone tomorrow"	Flexible schedules accommodating personal needs
Micromanagement	Management who appreciate and provide accurate feedback
A company which does not believe in long-term investment in Generation Xers	A cafeteria-style benefits package that values individual needs
General and insincere feedback and rewards	Regular staff meetings
	Feeling as if you make a difference
	A productive work atmosphere

Source: Vivian Yang, personal communication, Spring 1999

all workers and young workers suggest there is sentiment in favor of more balanced lives, requiring at least a modest shift from work to self and family. Employers might also expect young workers to want a different balance in their lives than older workers have chosen."[20] Assessing your workforce on these dimensions of preference would be an excellent way to get some sense of what your employees are thinking. One way to do that is to use the Index of Difference instrument introduced in Chapter Two.

■ The Total Compensation Solution, or the *New* New Pay

There are many changes on the horizon. Phrases like *variable pay, flattening base, cafeteria benefits, opportunities for growth*, and *psychic income* are common. Pay programs go by various names such as *nontraditional rewards, alternative reward strategies*, and *contemporary pay.*

Jay Schuster and Patricia Zingheim's 1992 book, *The New Pay*,[21] clearly recognized that old pay was not working. To quote the flyleaf of this important book: "Traditional pay, although professing to reward performance, is actually based on tenure, entitlement and internal equity. In contrast, the new pay practices . . . help form a positive partnership linking employee and organizational performance and providing employees with rewards that correspond to their own success and that of the organization. Viewing pay from the total compensation perspective, new pay ensures the most effective use of each component—base pay, variable pay (incentives) and indirect pay (benefits)."

Ed Lawler wrote the introduction to this book. He gave these initiatives the name "new pay," because the name "suggests that it will replace what now exists, rather than be a peculiarity that will pass with time. New pay is more than just business plan gainsharing, skill-based pay and employee involvement. The new pay view provides that organizations use all the elements of pay—direct cash (compensation) and indirect pay (benefits)—to help form a partnership between the organization and the employee. . . . New pay helps link the financial success of both the organization and its employees."[22]

Lawler had opened the door with his earlier work; Schuster and Zingheim walked through it. It was a pathbreaking stroll. They got three of the ten important variables in the total compensation solution. But as you can see from the Gen X chart in the preceding section, none of the things discussed in *The New Pay* were actually mentioned by this important group. Pay and benefits are necessary but not sufficient conditions for a compensation system.

The new new pay expands the idea of "total compensation" considerably, going beyond new pay in three important ways. The new new pay includes more variables than have been typically included in thinking about compensation. It also changes the basic assumption that compensation is an employer-driven element, positioning it as *employee* driven. The employee moves from being a recipient of pay to a customer of compensation. Customers, however, have to make choices. This is the third element of difference. There are trade-offs. If you sit down with a buddy over a beer and talk about the things you want from a workplace and the trade-offs you are willing to make for them, many, if not all, of these items will figure in that discussion. But you will not value all of them equally; you may want more base pay and less risk pay, or the reverse, or whatever. Cafeteria compensation allows for some of this trading to be done explicitly.

The Total Compensation Equation

The concept of the new new pay can be expressed in terms of an equation with ten variables. The equation is based on my research at the University of Michigan Business School—asking dozens of MBAs what they want from their workplace—as well as countless discussions with corporate executives and HR professionals. These ten variables represent the compensation package that is already implicitly present in most of our thinking. The problem is that it has not been organized in one place and presented as a unit, so it has been impossible to work with it effectively.

$$TC = (BP + AP + IP) + (WP + PP) + (OA + OG) + (PI + QL) + X$$

where

TC = total compensation
BP = base pay, or salary
AP = augmented pay, that is, any one-time payment, even if received at regular intervals (such as overtime)
IP = indirect pay (benefits)
WP = works-pay, that is, employer-subsidized equipment, uniforms, and so on
PP = perks-pay, that is, special benefits—anything from accessories to employee discounts on company products
OA = opportunity for advancement and increased responsibility
OG = opportunity for growth, both through on-the-job training and through off-site training and degree attainment
PI = psychic income, the emotional enhancements provided by the job itself and the setting (the people)
QL = quality of life, that is, opportunity to express other important aspects of life (location close to home, flextime, on-site child care, ski to work, or whatever)
X = any unique element that an employee wants that the workplace can facilitate ("Can I bring my dog to work?")

To borrow a phrase used conventionally with reference to external customers, this expanded view of compensation amounts to a "whatever it takes" approach to attracting, motivating, and retaining employees. Although increasingly comfortable with that approach with outside customers, employers have not applied this kind of thinking to internal customers, their employees. This larger view of what employees might want or need and the ways in which the employers can help will become a cornerstone of the compensation systems of the future. As Peter Capelli comments in *Harvard Business Review,* "Traditional strategies for employee retention are unsuited to a world where talent runs free. It's time for some fresh thinking."[23] For one thing, compensation strategy needs to have a threefold goal with respect to the workforce: encourage retention of the best (the top 20 percent), balance inflow and outflow of the middle mass (the middle 60 percent), and encourage departure of the rest (bottom 20 percent). Golden handcuffs will not hold the people you want to keep, because they are negated by golden hellos. Emphasis needs to be put on job design, job customization, good business location, and the encouragement of social ties. Capelli points out that people who will leave a company in a New York minute will hesitate to walk out on teammates. And Sue Shellenbarger, writing in the *Wall Street Journal,* titled one of her columns "An Overlooked Toll of Job Upheavals: Valuable Friendships."[24] Each of these items, and others, are addressed in the total compensation equation.

Capelli actually talks about Prudential's work on such an idea, and his observations are worth sharing: "In addition to tailoring jobs to particular categories of employees, companies can also tailor them to the needs of individuals. Prudential is experimenting with such a program. It provides workers with a variety of tools to help them assess their own interests, values and skills, and encourages managers to tailor rewards, benefits and assignments to individual requirements. A part-time arrangement might satisfy an employee's desire to pursue outside interests or meet a parenting need, while tuition reimbursement might be the key to keeping another employee happy."[25]

Prudential's program draws on an array of employment options, most of which are available to all workers. It's easy to imagine, however, programs that would go even further in customizing jobs. Key employees might undertake a formal self-assessment of their work and nonwork goals, and of how those goals could best be achieved in the context of the company's operations. The assessments would form the basis for individual employment agreements, which might be created using cafeteria-style programs similar to those used in allocating employee benefits. Each employee would be able to allocate a set amount of money toward options in such areas as career development and balancing work and personal life. The amount available to allocate would depend on the importance of the employee to the company. However, with this expanded list another important element comes into play. It is one thing to have different needs. It is another thing to have a system that allows you be able to make choices among them. That is where customization comes in.

Customization and Trade-Offs

Choice and *customization* are the watchwords of the 2000s. Everyone—Americans in particular—loves choice. We have choices among toothpastes, dog foods, dates, you name it. Choice itself has become a value. Hence the one-size-fits-all pay system of most companies is in need of upgrading.

Cafeteria benefits are perhaps the best example of this approach in today's workplace. Workers have an array of options from which to select—both within offerings (low-end to high-end medical coverage, for example) and among them (choosing, for example, between higher-end medical and long-term care insurance). A cafeteria benefits plan allows employees to build their own fringe benefits package, within limits.

Similarly, cafeteria compensation allows employees to build their own compensation package, and to change it at intervals (say, once a year) as their needs and interests change. The choice piece, however, also communicates to employees that there are trade-offs among kinds of compensation. Employers are asked to put the full package on the table, as they do in cafeteria benefits. The fact that employees need to pick and choose (as part of the customization process) among elements of the package educates them about the package and encourages them, rather than the employer, to make choices important to them.

The next chapter presents a more detailed view of these options and of the total compensation equation. For now, the bottom line is that over and above an expanded list of compensation dimensions, the new new pay allows employers to provide the gift of choice. And at least in America, that is a very valuable leverage.

CHAPTER SUMMARY

Cafeteria compensation—the new new pay—is a response to the need for diversity and choice in compensation programs. It is also a response to the intractable problems of old pay.

From the employer's perspective, old pay has several inherent problems that are compounded by the problems in old pay systems. Employees, too—particularly newer ones—may be satisfied with the money they receive and yet very dissatisfied with the pay system and the way pay information is communicated. Further, employees increasingly expect many other kinds of rewards besides dollars. The net result is that old pay no longer does the job of attracting, retaining, and motivating top-notch employees.

Even though employers may recognize many of these issues, there are several impediments to change. Among them are structural lag, means ritualism, and fundamental misunderstandings about employees. These issues become all the more serious in light of the changing nature of the workforce and the new demands and expectations of a diverse population of employees.

The total compensation equation addresses these issues by bringing all compensation elements together in a coherent package and introducing a degree of customization and choice into compensation. The model is cafeteria benefits—a once-radical solution that has achieved wide acceptance. Cafeteria compensation is responsive both to the changing workforce and to the failures of old pay from the employer's perspective. It is the direction in which compensation is moving and needs to move— whether all at once, or in incremental steps.

Cafeteria Compensation

The *New* New Pay

ay is one of the most important areas of the modern firm. It is what *compensates, drives, motivates,* and *rewards* employees for the work they do. Or it does the opposite of these things. Old pay—my term for most past and many current pay structures—winds up being a frozen structure based on tenure, entitlement, and internal equity. The concept of new pay began to articulate a more cogent direction for pay systems, linking pay to employee and firm success. New new pay, the concept introduced in this book, takes things a significant step further by combining the ideas of total compensation and employee choice.

The total compensation solution is based on four ideas. The first idea (explored in detail in Chapter One) is that previous and most current pay systems are a serious impediment to attracting, retaining, and motivating contemporary employees.

The second idea is that total compensation involves more than pay and benefits, or even rewards. It involves the ten variables of the total compensation equation: base pay, augmented pay (bonus, overtime, gainsharing), indirect pay (benefits), works-pay (tool allowances and so on), perks-pay (amenities and discounts), opportunity for advancement and growth, psychic income, quality of life (worklife versus whole life), and an X factor (any particular interest an employee may have).

The third idea is that these ten elements must be aligned in a solution tailored for each employee through a single organization—call it the Total Compensation Department. When the elements of total compensation are unaligned, firms lose leverage—even those that, at various places through their enterprise, pay attention to many, or all, of these variables.

The fourth idea is that the total compensation solution must involve some degree of choice for employees. It means that cafeteria compensation is on the way.

When I began articulating this approach in 1990, no one was doing anything like it. Now it is becoming more accepted. The American Compensation Association, in switching its name to "WorldatWork" with an expanded emphasis on "Total Rewards," did so for the same kinds of reasons important here. One is an increasing emphasis on things other than pay and benefits. The Total Rewards concept, the organization says, has three main components. Compensation (which I call base pay and augmented pay) and Benefits are two of them. The third is called the "Work Experience." Here is how WorldatWork puts it:

> "The Work Experience" includes the many elements of rewards that are important to employees and employers today but many times are less tangible. They overlap, relate to and

sometimes integrate with compensation and benefits. . . . The five key components of "The Work Experience" are

Acknowledgment, Appreciation and Recognition
Balance of Work/Life
Culture
Development
Environment[1]

The organization goes on to argue that it is the "collective impact of the components" that matters as much as the individual elements. Times are changing!

New new pay is a cafeteria compensation system that creates, first, a set of concepts for thinking about and administering total compensation, and second, an organizational place for one-stop shopping where all the variables that make up the compensations that employees expect are located. Accomplishing the transformation needed to implement the new new pay requires the following:

1. Deconstructing the idea of pay and reconstructing a philosophy of cafeteria compensation that helps us to understand all the parts of compensation
2. Using this understanding to build—reconstruct—a total compensation equation
3. Building a Total Compensation Department in which all elements of the compensation equation are located

This chapter completes the overview of the total compensation solution by examining these three key requirements. In Part 2, I'll examine each of the variables of the equation in detail. Those chapters will look at specific solutions to specific problems that move in the direction described here. In the language of Chapter One, these smaller solutions are transactional changes that an organization can make even if it is not prepared to take on the transformational change to a completely new compensation system.

■ The Philosophy of Cafeteria Compensation

Firms need a clear, coherent, and consistently articulated compensation philosophy. But they tend to have three problems when it comes to a pay philosophy: no philosophy, the wrong philosophy, or significant gaps between an appropriate philosophy and appropriate implementation.

Most organizations have no pay philosophy. (Some have a primitive one, such as the view shared by one older CEO: "We pay them to show up and shut up!") A good philosophy involves five key components:

- A clear understanding of what we pay employees for
- An understanding of what accomplishments we want from employees
- An understanding that employee compensation consists of both investments and rewards
- An understanding of the need to articulate the compensation philosophy in a compensation policy
- A compensation distribution matrix

As obvious as some of these points may seem, firms commonly stumble over some or all of them. It's worthwhile to consider each in turn.

1. What Do We Pay Employees *For?*

Few firms really know anything about their own compensation equation, or what you might call the compensation exchange. What, exactly, are they exchanging for what, exactly?

Surprisingly, many firms cannot even answer the question "What are we paying for?" I have asked managers around the country this question. The answers are instructive. I have already mentioned one typical example: "We pay employees to show up and shut up." Many other managers echo versions of this statement, though in more diplomatic terms. Another manager said, more or less, "What a stupid question. You've gotta pay people, for heaven's sake!" (His actual expression was a bit more colorful.)

But matters get worse. Firms that cannot articulate why they pay probably cannot articulate the work products they might pay for. Several years ago John Naisbett posed the question "What business are you in?"[2] This deceptively powerful query forces employers to ask themselves exactly what they are producing, offering, and selling. Then they can begin to answer the question of what they are paying employees to produce. Thus, the first step in defining rewards for employees is to ask what products the employees are supposed to produce, and what lines of business they are supposed to serve. That is a very difficult but necessary first step, and one that has benefits well beyond its contribution to compensation philosophy. This understanding is the score for the organizational orchestra; it allows all parts of the organization to achieve alignment so that each player is contributing in sync with all other players. In terms of the compensation system, it allows for desired employee accomplishments to be clearly articulated.

2. Accomplishment-Based Compensation

Cafeteria compensation is an accomplishment-centered system: employees are compensated based on their accomplishments on behalf of the organization. But without specifying what these accomplishments should be, a firm cannot compensate employees proactively, or at all, or with the right things. Once accomplishments become a set of results that employees need to produce, it can then compensate them through investments and rewards.

It is imperative to involve employees in this process. Employee *buy-in* to the accomplishment set cannot and will not be achieved without employee *build-in*. Accomplishments mean actually producing results. Accomplishments are outcomes driven, not process driven. For this to happen employees need to have a say in designing a structure of reasonable results. Then employees need to be assessed through the accomplishment ratio, the fraction of identified accomplishments each employee (or production unit, which can be a team) actually achieved. (Ratios can be below, at, or above 100 percent.)

3. Employee Investments and Rewards

Compensation is a two-part enterprise, consisting of both investments and rewards. Investments—sometimes called *prewards*—come before accomplishments and emerge as up-front dollars that are (supposedly) designed to pay off in the employee's and firm's future, and to create skills and motivation for accomplishment achievement. Rewards are paid after, and are (supposedly) contingent upon, accomplishments.

The center of the employer's awareness should be that investments and rewards sum to total compensation. The value of an investment is that it brings long-term high accomplishment, as the conventional phrase "the best investment I ever made" suggests. Rewards provide "post-accomplishment reinforcement" that completes the motivation cycle. In a compensation system, both investments and rewards are, or should be, accomplishment centered. That is, investments (pre-accomplishment compensation, or prewards) should be linked to accomplishments as much as rewards (post-accomplishment compensation, or *postwards*).

Both investments and rewards are necessary aspects of compensation. This observation means that human resources specialists are both stockbrokers and animal trainers.

On one hand, like stockbrokers, they need to create strategies to pick and motivate top talent (their "stocks") at the front end. Employees are like stocks in this one sense that we invest in them up front. (Creating and implementing employee investment strategies are among the tasks that we pay human resources to accomplish.) For each employee—or employee set (that is, the team)—there is a "payoff matrix" in which we invest a certain amount and expect a certain amount in terms of accomplishment.[3]

HR specialists, however, are like animal trainers as well as stockbrokers. They design and administer rewards at the back end of accomplishment. (One of the differences between dogs and people is that prewards do not work well with dogs.) Rewards can range from "thank you" for a job well done to large stock options when shareholder equity has been increased by a certain amount.

What has happened over time is that firms have forgotten the stockbroker model and seem to be shifting entirely to the animal trainer approach (the Milk-Bone model). They fail to understand compensation as an investment; they think of it as a cost. Investments are up-front elements of compensation that an employee is assured before accomplishing anything. Because employers regard these charges as costs rather than investments, they take the approach of trying to minimize them rather than manage them. That is the old pay mind-set. Employers, in effect, forget about the power of front-end compensation except in the aggregate budget of salaries and wages. As this number gets large, firms then "rightsize," reducing headcount (à la Chainsaw Al Dunlap) in order to "control costs."

Employers then put all their eggs in the rewards basket to motivate and retain. The recent rush to rewards in the form of bonuses is evidence of this. The popularity of rewards is built on top of the existing salary system rather than integrated or partnered with it. The result is that firms tend to look at strategies for "attracting, retaining, and motivating" as pay (bonuses, stock options, and so on) *beyond* the initial cost.

Figure 2.1 illustrates the flow between investments and accomplishments, and between accomplishments and rewards. Investments provide front-end motivation for accomplishments. This is the entering deal, and it needs to be redesigned yearly, with participation from employer and employee. Rewards provide back-end reinforcement for accomplishments, and employees similarly need to be involved in their design, overall and for themselves.

One advantage to the "front-end and back-end" compensation perspective is that it enables a full calculation of compensation returns. The full calculation looks at returns on compensation via accomplishment numbers. Investment ratios look at the front-end portion. Reward ratios look at the back-end portion. A competitive advantage today is to drive accomplishment through the roof through a front-back combo. Compensation analysis looks closely at the *ROC,* or "return on compensation," to see whether there actually is that kind of payoff. In old pay, the answer is often no, or, perhaps more frequently, "I have no idea; your guess is as good as mine."

Take an example from real estate. Real estate agents are not the most typical employees, but I think this example makes the point easy to understand as the difference between investment pay (salary and benefits) and reward pay (commission) is most clear for them. (Although I am talking investment *pay* and reward *pay* here for simplicity's sake, keep in mind that not all in-

---

INVESTMENT → **ACCOMPLISHMENT** → REWARD

Figure 2.1. Employee Compensation as an Investment-Reward Mix

vestment and reward compensation may be in dollars. It might be in opportunity for growth, perks, quality of life, and so on.) Say a real estate agent who works on a salary plus commission (investment plus rewards) sells $20 million worth of real estate in a certain year. The agent is paid $50,000 in salary and other forms of up-front compensation. That yields an investment ratio of 0.25 percent. Another agent, paid the same up front, sells only $3 million; that investment ratio is 1.66 percent. On the reward side, let's assume each gets 3 percent of their sales—$600,000 and $90,000, respectively. For the premier salesperson, that is an investment + reward ratio of $650,000/$20 million, or 3.25 percent. For the average salesperson, the same number is $140,000/$3 million, or 4.66 percent. Table 2.1 lays out these figures. The difference is obvious: the better agent is cheaper to employ, despite receiving a vastly larger income—and we have not factored in other employee expenses, such as the cost of an office.

A similar analysis could be made for other kinds of employees. For professors it might be grants received, students taught (or credit hours), dissertations successfully sponsored, or books and articles written.

Good businesspeople intuitively have a feel for these relationships, I think. In the case of Agent 2, one might be tempted to lower the reward; however, it might work better to lower the investment. The point is that we do not know what might work best for a particular employee. Cafeteria compensation, however,

Table 2.1. Investment and Reward Ratios for Two Real Estate Agents

	Investment Pay [A]	Sales [B]	Reward Pay (Commission) (3 percent) [C]	I-Ratio (A/B) [D]	R-Ratio (C/B) [E]	ROC (Return on Compensation) Ratio [F]
Agent 1	$50,000	$20,000,000	$600,000	0.25%	3%	3.25%
Agent 2	50,000	3,000,000	90,000	1.66	3	4.66

maximizes the possibility of targeting the employee's ideal pay-off matrix through customization. Giving each employee some chance to determine, in part, the way that they want to be paid has the greatest chance of providing maximum incentive, including both investment and reward considerations.

From the employee's point of view, investment compensation is less risky than reward-based compensation. It is like a fixed-rate mortgage. It is more reliable than reward-based compensation, but the opportunity for employees to gain through higher contribution is limited. Reward-based compensation is like an adjustable-rate mortgage: it is riskier and involves more uncertainty, but it also contains the potential for employees to make higher gains. Cafeteria compensation allows employees to combine these types of compensation in flexible ways to meet their own needs.

4. Articulating a Compensation Policy

Each firm needs to have a well-articulated, consistently administered compensation policy that embodies the firm's philosophy of compensation. Such a policy must meet several criteria:

- It is written.
- It is a guide to action.
- It has the approval of legitimate authority.
- It makes clear choices.

The distinction between compensation policy and compensation practice is the difference between what we write and what we do. All too frequently firms cite practice as policy. This tendency is yet another major problem with old pay. In the absence of policy, practice varies and is subject to wide interpretation and implementation.

Even with a policy, especially if it is a poor one, gaps develop between policy and practice. There will always be some gaps; indeed, analysis of policy/practice gaps provides firms with an excellent basis for policy refurbishment.

Employers and employees alike should be able to answer the question, What is the compensation policy at my shop? The cafeteria compensation answer involves several types of goals:

- Compensation is accomplishment-based.
- Compensation is made up of both investment and reward components.
- Compensation is employee driven; that is, within a defined range, the system is set up so that employees can customize their compensation package.
- Compensation policy successfully maintains the standard employee, rewards the exceptional employee, and encourages the subpar employee to leave.

To enlarge on that last point, the policy should send a strong message to employees at all levels of performance. Those who achieve accomplishment goals at par will find themselves paid at market; those who exceed par will be paid substantially above market; and those who achieve below par will be paid substantially below market.

In addition to these goals, effective compensation policies must include several elements. This aspect has been expertly outlined by Terry Satterfield.[4] He identifies six areas that compensation policy should address:

- Market position (lead/lag/mix)
- Pay mix (base vs. variable)
- Basis of job value (internal equity vs. market)
- Reward focus (collective vs. individual)
- Structure (traditional vs. broad bands)
- Administration (prescriptive vs. flexible)

Satterfield's article also gives a useful table of issues to consider in thinking about each of these areas. Good as it is, however, it does not mention *accomplishment*. Also, I am a little more prescriptive than he is, as my fourth goal suggests. Nonetheless, Satterfield presents an excellent starting list for a compensation policy.

Here is an example of a compensation policy for "High Quality Decisions," a firm that makes presentations on running better meetings. Its motto is "How to get as little done as you do now in half the time." Its employees consult on improving meeting culture, policy, and practice at firms around the world, making presentations on how to run more effective meetings and how to achieve higher-quality decisions in meetings.

The compensation policy at High Quality Decisions involves the following principles: It is made up of investments and rewards, and to a degree the company's associates can select more fixed compensation (investments) or more variable compensation (rewards) or sharing of firm profits (postwards). According to the company's stated policy, accomplishments at High Quality Decisions involve

- Achieving ratings of at least 4.3 out of 5 for each presentation (p)
- Securing repeat presentation business (r)
- Securing new presentation business (n)
- Securing consultation business (c)

The policy further states that investment compensation for associates is $50,000. For this the firm expects par performance of $p + r + n + c$. Associates, however, are *guaranteed* only $40,000 in investment compensation. The additional $10,000 is paid upon achievement of par performance on a quarterly basis. Achievement of better than par performance is compensated at an increasing rate: 10 percent better than par is compensated with one-time payments of 15 percent of the investment base, and 20 percent better than par at 25 percent of the investment base.

This example contains several elements that will be developed as we go along. Notice, for example, that although investment compensation (base salary) is fixed, it is also dependent on performance. Notice, too, the mix of investment compensation and one-time reward payments.

5. The Compensation Distribution

The distribution goal of total compensation for High Quality Decisions is based on the suggestions of Norman Harberger, a compensation consultant and principal of Harberger Associates, of Hilton Head Island, South Carolina. Employees are divided into three categories: the top 20 percent (suprapar), the middle 60 percent (par), and the bottom 20 percent (subpar). This distribution is a goal. The idea is to reward suprapar performers—those are the ones the company really wants to keep. They need money and recognition. The par performers are approximately at market, and are compensated accordingly. The pay philosophy also communicates to the subpar performers that they should leave. There is no golden handcuff here. Most managers would agree that, if you have ten employees, including two stars and two subpars, you can do better with the eight than with the ten, saving both managerial cost and the compensation cost for the two subpars. The distribution goal for compensation policy is summarized in Table 2.2.

■ The Elements of the Total Compensation Equation

The total compensation equation introduced in Chapter One is a structured response to old pay that fulfills the guidelines just described. It is at the heart of cafeteria compensation. Here is the equation again:

$$TC = (BP + AP + IP) + (WP + PP) + (OA + OG) + (PI + QL) + X$$

Table 2.2. Distributive Goals of Total Compensation

Employees	Observation	Cafeteria Compensation	Administrative Time Consumed
Top 20 percent	The real stars of the firm; we really seek to retain them. Their contribution far outweighs their cost.	Pay 20 percent or more above market.	Limited; communication on an as-needed basis; manager as a resource.
Middle 60 percent	Spear carriers; regular do-the-job employees. (Some might break this group into two: top 30 percent and bottom 30 percent.)	Pay at market to slightly above market.	Average; will vary by assignment.
Bottom 20 percent	Organizational drags. We wish to encourage them to leave.	Pay 10 percent to 20 percent below market.	Large; the firm could probably produce more if they were not present.

The issues associated with each of the variables in this equation are the subject matter of Part 2. Here is a closer look at what the variables represent.

First comes what most people think of as salary, or *pay*. In the total compensation equation, this is Base Pay (BP). Second is any overtime pay, stock options, gainsharing, or anything else employees might get on a one-time basis. This one-time basis could be regular—regular overtime, for example—but it is not guaranteed. That is Augmented Pay (AP). Third are "bennies," or fringe benefits, which I call Indirect Pay (IP). In the equation, these three items are grouped because they each represent "cash for you or on behalf of you" (true, some is cash now and some is cash later).

Fourth is works-pay (WP), which comprises an allowance for all those items—such as uniforms or tools—needed on the job that employees would otherwise have to purchase. Fifth is perks-pay (PP). Though declining, perks still are a motivator for some. Perhaps the most common perk is an employee discount on the firm's product. Works-pay and perks-pay are grouped because they represent cash that employees might spend for themselves on job-related elements (works-pay) or special features (discount on company products) that add value but are not, conventionally, considered compensation.

The sixth and seventh variables, opportunity for advancement (OA) and opportunity for growth (OG), address the issues of "room at the top" and opportunities to learn. Some employees want workplaces where they can move up quickly; others want workplaces where they learn either through on-the-job training or through employer support of training and degrees. These are bracketed because each refers to a type of career trajectory.

The eighth and ninth variables, psychic income (PI) and quality of life (QL), address the emotional rewards of the workplace and worklife/homelife balance issues.

Finally, X is that very personal factor that makes a difference to a particular employee—the thing that, if available, can make all the difference in attracting, retaining, and motivating that individual. Examples include bringing a dog to work, having access to massage therapy or car washing, getting a wine cellar moved, and other unique, personal things that can be make-or-break elements for a specific individual.

In thinking about a cafeteria compensation system, the first step is to get all the compensation—investment and rewards—in one place, conceptually and of course organizationally. The organizational part is called the Total Compensation Department.

The second step—the employee-driven part—is to allow employees to customize their rewards to some degree to meet their own needs. This customization may involve elements other than pay, such as opportunity for advancement or psychic income. This means that total compensation includes more than money, but it also means that the firm needs to handle these other needs in the context of money.

If you recall the Gen X matrix of turn-offs and turn-ons from Chapter One, other things than money were strongly present. This preference schedule means that other forms of compensation than money are available and desired. But often the nonmonetary elements are absent. In a sense, many firms overpay employees in cash because they do not have the wit and imagination—and the organizational structure—to create a compensation system that really works for the employee.

This is where the total compensation equation can introduce a refreshing clarity for employers and employees alike. A key feature of the equation is that the total compensation for a given employee is not only accounted for in one place, it is distributed differently depending on the employee's input. Total compensation represents 100 percent of the combination of investments and rewards. The employee can then elect to allocate portions of total compensation on a percentage basis to the ten variables according to that employee's needs and desires, within some range defined by the employer. So, for example, an employee who desires nothing in the way of perks can elect 0 percent for that variable and allocate the money to something that has a higher personal priority, such as quality of life (perhaps in the form of a slightly reduced work week, or the ability to work at home in the mornings). Or a particular employee who doesn't need health insurance (perhaps because he or she is covered by a spouse's insurance) can allocate the money that would otherwise be spent on insurance to some other variable, perhaps base pay. Or (again within limits) an employee might elect higher investment (base) pay and give up some potential rewards.

Viewing compensation in terms of this equation has several advantages. It broadens the kinds of things that have been traditionally thought about as compensation, and it connects them in one place. It allows us to see more clearly the trade-offs that employees make among elements of the equation as they go about making their decisions. It provides employees with a range of choices and an ability to customize, something that employers might not have considered in the past, and at the same time it allows employers to more accurately see what employees may want, and what the cost is to the employer.

Choice is becoming the key buzzword of compensation systems of the future. Choice means alternatives in terms of the range of things employees want from the workplace, and it also means alternatives in terms of the packaging of the compensation elements to meet personal needs at any given time and to change that mix as needs change over time. The total compensation equation expresses this dimension of choice.

■ The Total Compensation Department

The compensation equation is, so far, at the level of a thought process. Actually implementing it requires cultural change—a change in values—on several levels. Viewing compensation in this way involves significant rethinking about what pay is and how it should be administered.

We need to move beyond thought processes and even cultural change, however, to an organizational structure. To implement the total compensation idea, compensation and benefits staff and offices need to be thoroughly reorganized. In my view, the natural outcome of the concept of total compensation is a Total Compensation Department. This department is responsible for the recruitment, retention, and some of the motivation of employees. In scope and importance, its job will be very new and very challenging.

Cafeteria compensation specialists staff this department. The cafeteria compensation specialist works with each new employee to develop the kind of compensation package that would meet that employee's needs. With existing employees, the specialist works to keep the package updated as the employee's needs change. So, for example, a younger employee with children may want a higher-end benefits package with low doctor co-pays. An older employee, with fewer or no kids and more money, may not mind higher co-pays. That same older employee may prefer to save more for retirement, having less need for cash now and more potential need for cash later.

Some of these kinds of actions can already be taken by employees. But the process tends to be largely random, and in large organizations requires a lot of employee initiative. Hence the employer is not leveraging the system or getting the benefits of the goodwill that comes from reaching out to meet employees' needs.

One of the ways a firm can capitalize on benefits is by helping employees understand what it is they really want and value. A way to do that is to employ the Index of Difference, an instrument that measures the gap between an employee's real and desired state (see Table 2.3).

The Index of Difference allows us to calculate how different what employees want is from what they have. For this example I am using a "life balance" approach. I urge you to try it,

Table 2.3. The Index of Difference for an Imaginary Employee

Arena of Life	Sample			Your Turn		
	Ideal A	Actual B	Difference |A–B|	Ideal A	Actual B	Difference |A–B|
Work (%)	25	100	75			
Family (%)	25	0	25			
Self (%)	25	0	25			
Civic (%)	25	0	25			
TOTAL (%)	100	100	150	100	100	
Index			150/2=75			Sum/2=

Note: You're invited to use the "Your Turn" columns to see how your own index looks.

and get a feel for how this tool works. Then there will be a chance to apply it to the ten-variable cafeteria compensation equation.

Let's assume there are four areas of life in which you seek balance—time for work, for your family, for civic activities (church, associations, and so on), and some for yourself. You have only 100 percent of your time to give, so, somehow, that 100 percent must be divided among those four areas, giving relative emphasis to one or the other. In this case, the hypothetical employee wishes to spend 25 percent of the time in each area, as shown in Column A—but (working for Overwork.com) actually spends all available time at work and none in any of the other areas, as shown in Column B. The third column shows the absolute difference between each row in the first two columns (*absolute difference* means disregarding plus and minus signs, that is, whether the calculated difference is positive or negative). The summed absolute difference (150 percent, in this case) is then divided by 2. Our hypothetical employee thus has an index of difference of 75, and is thus 75 percent out of whack!

Note that "out of whack" means that this employee's wishes and actual situation are very different. This approach does not tell us what is right and wrong. Perhaps the ideal distribution needs reexamination. On the other hand, perhaps the ideal distribution makes good sense, and the employee has drifted into an actual situation that must be very uncomfortable. Understanding the differences is one thing; looking for the source of the differences is a second thing; thinking, and then acting, to create greater alignment is the last thing. Generally, the index should be 10 or below to achieve "fit." In the next three columns you can try it yourself.

The Index of Difference tells us how different what someone wants is from what he or she has, and where the differences lie. The same technique can be applied to the specific realm of compensation via what I call the Compensation Assay (see Table 2.4).

Table 2.4. **The Compensation Assay for an Imaginary Employee**

Arena of Life	Sample			Your Turn		
	Ideal A	Actual B	Difference |A–B|	Ideal A	Actual B	Difference |A–B|
Base pay (%)	30	70	40			
Augmented pay (%)	50	00	50			
Indirect pay (%)	00	30	30			
Works-pay (%)	00	00	00			
Perks-pay (%)	00	00	00			
Opportunity for growth (%)	10	00	10			
Opportunity for advancement (%)	00	00	00			
Psychic income (%)	05	00	05			
Quality of life (%)	00	00	00			
X factor (%)	05	00	05			
Total (%)	100	100	140	100	100	
Index			140/2=70			Sum/2=

Note: You're invited to use the "Your Turn" columns to see how your own assay looks.

The Compensation Assay allows us to calculate how different what employees want is from what they have in terms of their total compensation. In Column A employees put down the proportions they would ideally like to allocate to the various elements of the total compensation equation. Of course, these proportions must total to 100 percent, the sum of all available compensation. In Column B the employee (with the help of the compensation specialist) places the current compensation fractions. The third column once again shows the absolute difference of the first two columns, and the summed absolute difference is again divided by 2. The resulting number—the index of difference as applied to compensation—reveals exactly how different what the employee wants is from what the employee currently has and where the differences lie.

The compensation assay is the operational mechanism for the compensation equation. There are several uses for this assay.

The first use is for the firm itself. The firm needs to take this assay, to look at what it is doing in comparison to what it wants to do. The "ideal" in this case is compensation policy, what the firm wants to do, which may be difficult to figure out. The "actual" part may be equally difficult, trying to find out what the firm really offers at present. Here the point is to assign ranges to each variable, rather than exact percentages, since the idea is to give employees a chance to elect percentages within a prescribed range.

This process may seem complex, but many firms have already had a preliminary run-through. If your firm has gone to cafeteria benefits, you have essentially completed the first step with respect to benefits. There, one has to decide what kinds of benefits to offer (ideal), what benefits are currently being offered (actual), and what the range of employee election is going to be. This means that a *benefits policy* has been articulated, and a *payout/choice matrix* established.

What does it mean for the firm to take the assay? As a practical matter, a random sample of employees would fill out the assay, a sample drawn such that an overall index can be established, and indices by unit, region, level—various important organizational breakdowns—can also be articulated.

At this point, the firm can get a sense of the degree to which its compensation practices, as currently offered, meet employee needs. One example came from a recent seminar I gave on this material—at the "Growing the Organization" conference at the University of Michigan's Executive Education Center in Ann Arbor, in July 2000. About fifteen executives were in the room, and I asked them to fill out the assay. Overwhelmingly they wanted greater quality of life, for which they would accept less pay. But each said it was impossible to achieve that in their firm! You can see the opportunities that the organization is giving up through not having this information.

The information allows the firm to do a couple of things it should do, but usually does not. The first is to see where the organization actually is, with respect to the needs and desires of its employees. The second is to see where it wishes to be. This "wish to be" piece becomes the first cut at a compensation policy and the first part of the payout/choice matrix. A second part of the payout matrix is to figure out what the range of choices for cash and noncash areas would be. I have suggested some in Table 2.4. Cash and noncash areas also need to be decided. Base pay, augmented pay, and benefits are key cash areas, and have flexibility within them. (If my wife's benefits are great, I can elect no benefits from my firm, converting 50 percent of mine to cash.) But others, such as perks, may or may not be cash or have cash elements.

The elements of works-pay, perks-pay, opportunities for growth and advancement, psychic income, quality of life, and the X factor require organizational decisions about what are the minimum packages for each job class, and whether or not premium upgrades will be allowed. For example, everyone at a retail company may be allowed a 20 percent discount on purchases from the store. However, a particular employee might wish to select an additional percentage of total compensation that can be applied toward charges. I have provided for that in my example. Similarly, a firm usually has "packages" of equipment that it will provide for new employees (uniforms, desks, tools, and so on). Then there is desirable equipment (extra weapons for cops, special tools for airline mechanics, special computer outfitting) for which extra support is wished. Here again, in my example, an elective amount is allocated there. In each of these two cases, that money can be available as cash if the employee prefers.

In some cases, say quality of life, there may be a mix. For example, one aspect of quality of life for many employees is on-site child care (where they can watch their kids in the facility through a monitor!). This may cost $1,000 per month. The employee has to buy it, but is still glad to have it. Or take parking. At the University of Michigan I have to pay for my own parking sticker, but the department chips in something.

Some benefits may not be convertible for cash. For example, consider a firm that will support an employee's getting an MBA degree at an elite school. Assuming the employee gains admission, the tuition might run as high as $40,000 to $50,000 per year. The firm might decide it is a good idea to support the acquisition of this degree (up to this amount; less elite schools and on-line schools are less expensive), but an employee who does not meet company criteria cannot convert the support into cash.

Of course, firms may use any kind of policy they choose. The point is that the compensation equation forces the organization to develop a comprehensive compensation policy, looking carefully at what it wants to provide.

Beyond its use in the planning and research necessary to develop a compensation policy, the compensation assay has individual uses as well. Let me mention three of them. One is in the recruitment phase. Recruiters can use it to see how to customize offers to employees. Second, employees can use the assay as a preliminary assessment each year as they prepare to reevaluate the compensation array. Third, HR specialists can use it in career planning, including outplacement decisions.

All of this activity is designed to assist the firm in becoming an employer of choice, something good for the employer and good for the employee. One of the keys to becoming the employer of choice in today's marketplace is a flexible compensation system that allows for a diversity of employee needs while serving the company's goal of achieving a good return on employee investment. Table 2.5 shows a range of possible systems and grades them according to their likely efficacy in terms

Table 2.5. How to Become the Employer of Choice

System Grade	Comment
F	Take it or leave it; system is completely rigid. Nonchanging system.
D	Take it, but if you protest we might make some small adjustments; system is mostly rigid. Episodically reactive.
C	Take it or move to another department; system is rigid but some variation in individual managers' application of the system. The firm is reactive as a whole, but departmentally proactive.
B	Employee needs are anticipated to a degree; system is proactive.
A	Employee is surprised and delighted! Employee needs are met beyond expectations. Employer of choice.

of attracting, retaining, and motivating employees. The system that gets an "A" is the total compensation system of the future, one that treats employees as internal customers.

CHAPTER SUMMARY

The total compensation equation brings together in one place the elements that go into a comprehensive solution. Underlying this approach is a philosophy of compensation that is accomplishment-based and that allows for an appropriate and customized balance of investments and rewards.

A key advantage of this approach is that it takes in nonmonetary compensations that many newer workers value, and that can be just as motivating as cash. Further, this approach makes trade-offs and costs clearer to employee and employer alike. And, what is most important, it allows for a significant degree of employee customization and choice.

The Index of Difference and the Compensation Assay are instruments that can help both organizations and individuals quantify the gap between what they desire and what they have, and tailor solutions accordingly. In a thoroughly redone compensation system, the Compensation Assay would be a key tool for employees and compensation specialists. Even short of such a transformation, it can serve as an analytical tool to organize thinking about compensation and clarify the intermediate steps an organization might want to take to modernize its compensation system.

The journey to a new system can be done in steps or in leaps—or in one big leap. Part 2 examines the individual variables in the total compensation equation and suggests improvements that firms can make, either singly or in combination, to move toward a system that will better serve the interests of both employer and employee.

The Total Compensation Equation

I n the chapters in Part 2 we'll explore each of the ten terms of the total compensation equation. Taken together, these variables represent all the parts of a compensation package that need to be taken into consideration by compensation managers. Recall that I am arguing here for a single, integrated department—a conductor who can direct the pieces of the compensation orchestra depending on the score being played (the employee). Nevertheless, each term of the equation has its own issues that deserve separate examination.

As we go through each term, I will use a common format for the chapter. Following the introduction of the topic, a "Problems" section will detail the issues associated with the particular compensation element being discussed. That section will be followed, logically enough, by one titled "Suggested Solutions."

We begin with the first term in the total compensation equation, base pay. This is the most common form of what is commonly called "salary" or "pay." For most companies it represents the most costly part of the compensation orchestra. For most employees, it has multiple meanings.

The Battle of Base Pay

The Security of Salary

We Americans are a garrulous lot. We will talk about anything to almost anyone—cab drivers, researchers, the guy next to us on the bus. Researchers are fond of telling stories about interviewing subjects who casually admit to bizarre sexual practices and even felonies (or make that felonies and even bizarre sexual practices). There's just one exception: money. Researchers usually put questions about income at the end of a questionnaire, because it is so often a turn-off. Money has become the great American secret. There may be a millionaire next door, but you might not know it.[1]

This sensitivity to money reflects its odd combination of practical and quasi-spiritual value. Two questions keep coming up, and becoming intermingled: What does money buy? and What does money mean?

■ What Money Buys, What Money Means

At one level, of course, money buys resources that one needs to live. Years ago, in producer societies, people grew, raised, or made most of those resources on their own farms. If there was a surplus, it was sold for money, but the money was something extra. Today we all work for money, and anything we produce—from a small vegetable garden, say—has become the extra. We have moved from a producer society to a consumer society. Now we buy our resources with money. We need a cash income to meet our routine obligations.

That is not all that money buys, however. Guaranteed money—a wage or salary—buys reassurance. It's as if farmers were promised year upon year of perfect soil and weather. Hence, money in the form of salary represents resources for both the here-and-now self and the then-and-there self.

Even at the material level, "what money buys" includes both needs and wants. Needs, of course, are the necessities of daily life. Wants go beyond necessities and can emerge into what the economist Thorstein Veblen called "conspicuous consumption" a century ago.[2] Today we are moving from the utilitarian individualism (buying useful products) of our past to today's expressive individualism (buying products that express our inner selves). Display rather than utility is the order of the day.

It is at this point that we slide into the second question, What does money mean? Money buys something more than material goods; it buys *products* that are, in part, emotional (this point connects with the idea of psychic income introduced earlier). Money buys respect—self-respect and respect from others. In the historical American value system, the richer person is the better person, even if we don't always say so out loud. Money means "I'm OK," "I'm a success." More money means that I am *more* of a success.

In a sense, a salary is our personal work product. We don't usually get to take home the products and services we contribute to making, but we do have "take home" pay. One view of meaningful work is that it is any well-paid work. It is from its connection to work that money derives its quasi-sacred status.

And here is the connection to the battle of base pay. Base pay provides more than the income base. In fact, it could more accurately be called *most pay,* since, for most employees, it makes up most of the compensation. Employees associate a sense of security, and then entitlement, to the "most pay" they get.

Because employees' sense of worth has become attached to this "most pay," moving from that position of entitlement to accomplishment-based pay presents a number of problems that companies must face. Let's take a look at some of the issues base pay presents, and then explore ways we might deal with them.

■ The Problems

Pay is a battleground in part because it is highly visible. In the past twenty years employers have struggled to increase productivity, offer better quality, and gain control of their costs. *Faster, better, cheaper* has been the mantra in every kind of organization. Because payroll is a large, visible, and malleable part of the product cost, one important tool in this enterprise has been reducing headcount—downsizing, resizing, rightsizing, whateversizing. Of course, you can only reduce headcount up to a point, and then you run the risk of throwing the baby out with the bathwater. Ultimately, employers realized that they were throwing out the very resource that could make them achieve the goal of faster, better, cheaper.

The fashion for headcount reduction came from one of the problems with pay that I noted earlier: the mind-set that employees equal cost and hence that to reduce employee numbers is to reduce cost. The approach is simplistic rather than simple. It provides a quick fix rather than a root-cause solution. Employees, in fact, are—or should be—investments rather than costs. As a practical matter, if you work for me, I really don't care how much I pay you; what matters is how much profit you produce for me. Consider *Fortune*'s "Manager of the Century," Jack (Neutron Jack) Welch, who oversaw a market-value increase for General Electric from $13 billion in 1981 to $425 billion today, a 3,269.23 percent increase.[3] I'll take it. If you're GE, do you care how much you pay him? Not as long as it's proportionate to the profit he brings you. But that, of course, is not how employers generally think about pay.

Attitudes, Organizational Structures, and Resistance to Change

Apart from pay's visibility, the question of base pay has three main problem areas. The first concerns the amount of money that employees feel they deserve, the money the employers actually pay, and the separation of both from individual and organizational results and accomplishments. Employee and employer attitudes, hardened into corporate structures, are the twin rocks on which many plans for change founder. This point is related to some of the problems I have already mentioned, including annuitization and the mentality of entitlement.

The second part of the problem lies in poor organization of the pay system. In spite of the fact that compensation costs are a large fraction of most business operations, neither employees nor employers have thought of compensation as a total package. Employers may have routinely read reports purporting to show total compensation costs, but employees most certainly lacked the idea of total compensation as something for which they worked. Benefits, in particular, were not seen by employees as pay.

In reality, neither party had a firm grasp on the concept of total compensation. Rather, compensation was broken up into components: base pay, fringe benefits, bonuses, overtime, perks, allowances. It was difficult at best to get all the numbers in one place. Further, these components were often administered by different parts of the organization. Base salary was determined under one unit of the organization, using one set of principles. Benefits were developed and administered under another department using different rationales and philosophies. Bonuses and special pay were in yet another place, or at least for all intents and purposes administered independently. The third part of the problem lies in moving the mountains—changing or altering the base-pay concepts of both employers and employees in such a way that firms can move to a less rigid, more nimble system.

Constructing Base Pay

Any rethinking of pay needs to confront the fundamental issue of how base pay should be constructed. Over the years, employers have tried a number of approaches to constructing base pay. The three major ones can be characterized as pay the job, pay the person, and pay the results. None is free of issues.

Pay the Job

In the pay-the-job approach, the characteristics of the person do not matter much. The system used here is the so-called point-factor system; for years it dominated the pay systems of many American corporations.

The point-factor system rates jobs by compensable factors (for example, skill, mental effort, responsibility) and builds a salary out of them. It is intended to ensure that jobs are paid fairly with respect to one another based on the proportion of the compensable factors they contain.[4] A corollary is that bands of jobs should be developed representing a certain range of points.

Naturally, this system resulted in long lists of jobs at many companies (and in the federal government). This approach had the obvious strengths of objectivity and impersonality. However, because pay was tied to jobs, the system promoted lying about the nature of jobs to get employees into the next grade; apart from the annual raise, moving up in the point system was the only way to get more money. Perhaps more seriously, it did not really ask whether anyone actually produced anything, and it did not distinguish well between high and low performers. Finally, the pay-the-job approach tended to ignore other things one might wish to compensate, such as developing skills, minimizing scrap, achieving results, attaining degrees, and so on.

Pay the Person

The pay-the-job system excludes the person. This, of course, is hard on the person. In recognition of this exclusion, employers developed alternative methods that took into account individuals' skills and knowledge. "Pay for knowledge" took account of the educational level that an employee brought to the job. "Pay for skills" provided additional money for new competencies learned on or through the job. Employers liked this approach because it rewarded employees for becoming more broadly capable. However, difficulties arose because employees sometimes never got to use their new skills; furthermore, skills become obsolete. Either way, the major problem with both these approaches is that pay can quickly become separated from results.

Pay the Results

Results-based pay ignores inputs (the job, the employee) and looks only at the output: outcomes, or results. Under this system, people with very different qualifications and training might have the same output and, hence, the same pay. Commission-based compensation is the perfect example. If I'm supposed to sell cars, then the boss's only question is, "How many did you sell?"

While seeming to be ideal, this approach has a number of problems. Pay for results ignores the setting. For example, as was dramatized in *Glengarry Glen Ross*, the 1992 film about high-pressure condo salesmen, individuals might be given more or less attractive properties to sell, or more or less lucrative client lists. Thus, pay for results not only ignores the person but can introduce new inequities.

Variations and Refinements

There are a number of refinements to the three basic approaches to pay just described. Table 3.1, which appeared in a publication of the American Compensation Association, provides a handy summary.

The overarching problem is that none of these systems really works well, or well enough. Each has its advantages in some settings, but, as the table indicates, each also has its own set of problems. New approaches are needed to address some of the fundamental issues revolving around base pay.

■ **Suggested Solutions**

Several base pay improvements, all consistent with the total compensation philosophy, can be part of an overall solution to the challenge of compensation. Three of the suggestions I review here—broad-banding, variable pay, and the split increase—deal with restructuring pay itself. The remaining two suggestions address organizational and systemic issues. These are approaches that firms are already taking, and they add positive elements into the administration of base pay.

Table 3.1. Approaches to Base Pay

Approach	Attributes	Challenges
1. Automatic step progression (pay the job)	■ Easy to administer and explain ■ Particularly appropriate for task-oriented, short-cycle jobs that do not require interpersonal skills ■ Ensures cost control at no more than market rate ■ Title VII/EPA Compliance	■ Does not address cooperation and teamwork ■ Can allow managers and supervisors to abdicate their performance management responsibility
2. Merit range (pay the job)	■ Allows flexibility to customize performance measures ■ Allows for significant base rate differences based upon sustained performance ■ Range of pay per grade can be more responsive to market pressures in particular job families	■ Assumes managers and supervisors are capable of making distribution decisions ■ Difficult or even impossible to reduce base rates that are high in range ■ Performance measurement pressures ■ Title VII/EPA Compliance
3. Skill-based pay (pay the person)	■ Focuses employees on skill acquisition ■ Identifies clear development paths for employees to pursue ■ Ensures employees with broadest skill profiles are rewarded	■ Very individually focused and can be a barrier to teamwork ■ Administrative burden ■ Skill/job obsolescence ■ Per-employee cost of labor higher than traditional approaches
4. Competency-based pay (pay the person)	■ Focuses employees on developing breadth and depth of knowledge ■ Provides "person based" versus "job based" methodologies ■ Provides analysis that leads to competency identification and ensures alignment with business needs	■ Administrative burden ■ Skill/job obsolescence ■ Per-employee cost of labor can become high relative to traditional pay delivery systems ■ Translating "job-based" market data to "person-based" work environment

Table 3.1. Approaches to Base Pay, cont'd

Approach	Attributes	Challenges
5. Team-based pay (pay the results)	• Reinforces that the whole is greater than the parts • Shared risk and reward • Assumes high level of trust across teams • Relatively easy to administer • Easy to communicate	• Employee "shopping" for the team that best fits their needs • Doesn't focus on the individual's personal development • Difficult to administer when there is fluidity of project assignments (i.e., who is on the team?) • Title VII/EPA compliance especially if and when teams become segregated
6. Lump sum distribution (pay the results)	• Allows lump sum to reward performance one time versus forever • Reduces costs of associated benefits because of the lower pay base annuity per employee • Title VII/EPA compliant • No merit increase matrix	• Difficult to institutionalize • Extreme pressure on performance measurement and evolution • FSLA "regular rate" requirements for nonexempt • High labor rate inflation may be difficult to manage and explain

Source: John Breneman and Maggi Coil, "Comparing Alternative Base Pay Methods." *ACA News* (June 1999): 21–25, Figure 7.

Broad-Banding

One step toward change already taken by many firms is broad-banding. This approach, which involves collapsing long lists of jobs into broader bands, is an attempt to address some of the difficulties of extensive job categories that the pay-the-job approach created. It also provides a way around the potential lockstep of the point-factor system.

Variable Pay

A second approach is to reconsider what the firm guarantees the employee in terms of pay. Let's say an employee's base pay is $50,000. In the past, that employee would simply have received the $50,000. In a variable pay scheme, an employee with a salary of $50,000 is guaranteed, say, $35,000. The employee reaches the $50,000 level only by achieving certain agreed-upon objectives, or, in our terms here, *accomplishments.* In addition, the employee can stretch the amount of pay to, say, $65,000 by exceeding the agreed-upon accomplishment levels (see Figure 3.1). This approach addresses a concern of employers who often feel that, although they are committed to pay the employee, the employee is not committed to achieving any results for that pay.

In this example, someone theoretically making $50,000 would be guaranteed $35,000 and be eligible for the remaining $15,000 if certain goals were met. The employee could become eligible for an additional $15,000 by meeting certain additional goals. These goals are mutually agreed to at the beginning of the "compensation season."

Variable Merit, or the Split Increase

So-called merit increases typically go into the base pay. This is the problem of annuitization mentioned earlier: as an employer, you are paying for last year's productivity for as long as the em-

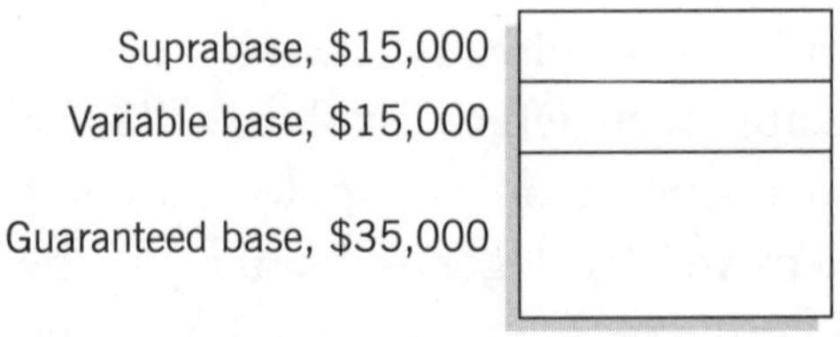

Suprabase, $15,000
Variable base, $15,000

Guaranteed base, $35,000

Figure 3.1. Illustrative Display of a Variable Pay Package of Base, Variable Base, and Suprabase

ployee is with you. Hence, employers have tried to keep merit increases down, thus irritating the best employees. They have also tried to limit the ability to provide raises by establishing salary "ranges" for each job grade. When employees reach the top of their particular grade, they are told, "Sorry, there is nothing anyone can do." This answer further irritates outstanding workers, who are likely to get to the top of the range faster than less effective workers. It also stimulates job up-spinning, whereby Ed's job (editor) is spun into "senior editor" and then "executive editor" in order to get Ed some additional dollars.

A better system is suggested by Don Lowman of Towers Perrin, who was introduced in Chapter One. It is outlined in Table 3.2. Let's say that Ed's salary range is between $40,000 and $50,000, making $45,000 the range midpoint. Let's also say that for the current year the company has announced a raise, for Ed's job class, of between zero and 10 percent. That means that the midpoint of the raise range is 5 percent. The idea here is that if Ed is below (or at) either of the two midpoints (the lower right quadrant), everything he gets will go into his base. But if he is above the salary midpoint and gets an above-average award, say 10 percent, then half of the increase goes into his base and half becomes a one-time payment. (These discriminator numbers need not be the midpoint, by the way—they can be set at any value within the award and salary ranges.) If he is at the salary

Table 3.2. The Split Increase Method of Allocating a Raise Partially into Base and Partially into Lump Sum Payments

	Position in Salary Range	
Percent Increase	Top Half	Bottom Half
Top half	Split or lump sum*	Split
Bottom half	Split	Into base

Note: Split = split between lump sum and base. In this example, the range and increase values for partitioning have been set at their respective midpoints. These values could, of course, be set at any values over the respective ranges, changing the shape of the lower quadrant.

*A person who is already at the top of his or her salary range would receive the entire increase in a lump sum.

maximum for his range ($50,000) and receives the highest allowable award (10 percent), under this system he will get a check for $5,000. Nothing will go into the base. (Note the use of *award* instead of *raise* or *increase*. Historically, the latter words are associated with an 'attached to the base' mind-set, and it's useful to have a new term for the new, flexible reality.) Adding nothing to the base may make it look as though Ed is getting cheated of the sort of reward he'd get under the current system, but it means he can get the same award next year, regardless of his income, if his performance warrants it. In the typical system, such a high performer could get no raise at all because he would be at the top of his range. How foolish, and what a wonderful idea this approach is by contrast!

Pay Alignment—Vertical and Horizontal

At the level of structure, an important way to improve pay is to align it both vertically and horizontally along the dimensions shown in Table 3.3. Vertically, the cells in the three columns need to be tightly connected. In Table 3.3, the first column refers to the level of the firm—the top executives, the broad middle line, and the individual employee. Each has a certain relationship to pay. At the top level, the job of the executive is to articulate why the firm pays—a pay policy—and set up the various dimensions of pay, something which I have called *pay architecture.* It's as if you

Table 3.3. The Vertical and Horizontal Pay System Alignment Grid

Macro: Top team level	Pay vision and values ("Why we pay")	Total compensation architecture
Meso: HR level	Pay goals and strategy ("How we pay")	Total compensation array
Micro: Employee level	Pay objectives and tactics ("How your pay is constructed")	Employee package

Note: This grid displays the elements of pay that need to assume a "tight fit." Tight fit both across the rows and up and down the columns is essential for a coordinated pay system.

were building a house. "House policy" would be your articulation of what the house should do, and what needs it should meet. "House architecture" is the plans for it.

In the middle row we have the "contractors" developing a strategy to build the house (middle managers making pay "work" or not) and the array of compensation opportunities that are available in this plant or that one. The contractors have their own strategy derived from the architect's rendering.

Finally we have the individual employee, what each one winds up getting. This would be the detail: what the kitchen is like, what the garage is like, and whether they meet the user's needs.

What is important is that Columns 2 and 3 be "tight." Look, for example, at the middle column. Pay vision and values need to drive pay goals and strategy, which in turn need to drive pay objectives and tactics. In other words, organizations need to talk the talk, and then walk the talk at the policy level.

There should be upward flow as well, with issues and problems at the tactical level influencing changes at the strategic level, which in turn influence change in vision and values. This means that the firm should listen to employees on an ongoing basis, and update and enhance its pay policy based on input from the payees. In the *new* new pay, the architecture of total compensation drives the total compensation array, from which each employee configures a personal pay package.

Pay Change

Changing pay delivery systems is a complicated process. As I discussed in Chapter One, pay culture is deeply entrenched in the mind-sets of both employer and employee. Although the distinction depicted is obviously an oversimplification, Table 3.4 outlines some of the issues in pay—the pay problem, the challenge of change, the pace of change, and the kind of change—as a function of the age of a firm and the typical age of its workers.

Table 3.4. The Problems of Pay, the Challenge of Change, the Pace of Change, and the Kind of Change, Considering Age of Workforce and Age of Firm

Age of Workforce	Age of Firm	
	Young	**Mature**
Young	Problem: Establishing a pay system Challenge: Designing the pay system and fine-tuning it Pace: Rapid Kind: Modulating	Problem: Traditional employer attitudes about pay Challenge: Firm culture and structure change in the face of young workers Pace: Moderate Kind: Transactional
Mature	Problem: Traditional employee attitudes about pay Challenge: Retooling older workers with hardwired values and perspectives Pace: Rapid Kind: Transactional	Problem: Double lock of dated but synchronous employer-employee attitudes Challenge: Cataclysmic event often required Pace: Very slow and perhaps nonexistent; the firm may die Kind: Transformational

Let's start in the lower right quadrant—the older firm with the older workforce, typical of many companies today. The longer a culture has been operative, the tougher it is to change. Here both employer and employee attitudes are traditional ones. Transformational change—change of the system—is what is needed. Small, incremental changes will not work because of the overall resistance. The tough part is that transformational change—revolution over evolution—may not occur unless there is a force from outside.

The lower left and upper right cells have similar problems—either employer or worker attitudes and practices. Here transformational change—evolution or change in the system—is possible, because there is likely to be a mix of support and opposition. Older employers are less willing to share the wealth and frequently covet the gains—all the gains—made by workers. As

I mentioned, they are more likely to view employees as a cost and to seek, as they have been taught, to minimize all cost. Older employees, meanwhile, have often lived through hard times; furthermore, they know the orientations of older employers. Consequently, they are more prone to seek the security of good base pay. (Many believe that employers will not share the wealth anyway.) In short, older workers tend to believe that more base pay is better and means they are more successful; older employers tend to believe that less base pay is better and that if they pay too much they are being taken advantage of. In "mixed cases" (young firms with old employees, or the reverse), only half of the problem is present. Of course, the approach will be different depending on whether the target of change is the employer or the employees.

In the upper left cell—young workers and a young firm—pay systems are often in flux and variegated. One of the owners of Zingerman's Delicatessen in Ann Arbor, a very successful young firm with many young workers, told me, "I do not really care how I pay people—I let them pick; I have given people two plans—one with more base and less risk, and the reverse—and asked them to pick." In such settings, change is rapid and of a modulating kind. Because the pay system has less baggage, it can be—and often is—more flexible and more regularly updated than is true at older firms or firms with more traditional workers.

Clearly, change efforts must be tailored to the situation. In any such effort, however, it can help to build in the five I's:

- Ideas
- Input
- Involvement
- Information
- Improvement

To begin with, a change effort requires *ideas*. Some, of course, can be acquired from consultants, from books, or even from professors. Some of the best ideas, however, are likely to come from those closest to you: your workers.

This leads to *input*. Any system design needs input from those it affects. What is important to your workers? What genuinely motivates them? (Recall the "Index of Difference" instrument introduced in Chapter Two.)

Next, it is essential to design for *involvement* in the administration of the plan by its recipients. The approach I recommend here is an example; in cafeteria compensation, employees are involved in designing and modifying, within limits, their own compensation packages. Even prior to a cafeteria compensation plan, however, employee involvement is needed in telling employers what kinds of compensation they want, and what kind of mix and choices would please them.

Information relates to the constant need to communicate the plan. New employees—including managers—continually enter the firm. They need to have the nature and structure of the pay system communicated to them up front, and the message needs to be reinforced for all employees on a regular basis. The way pay plans are communicated has an independent effect over and above the substance of the plan. If this doesn't seem obvious, think of a typical set of experiences in a restaurant. An average meal, superbly served, may yield greater satisfaction than an excellent meal, grudgingly served by a haughty waiter.

Continual *improvement* is not just something for the folks who design "Total Quality" programs. As the environment shifts quickly, so must compensation plans. They need to have nimble changeability designed in. Again, this is an intrinsic part of the cafeteria compensation approach.

CHAPTER SUMMARY

In this chapter we have considered the battle of base pay, or "most pay." The battle is not just about numbers. Pay buys some things, and it also means other things to individuals. For these reasons, it becomes something of a sacred cow and very difficult to approach, especially in older firms with older workers.

The problems with base pay, though, create pressures for change. Pay is visible, and hence becomes a target for cutting, even if cutting pay is not, as it might seem, the best (or even a good) strategy. When employers think that employees equal cost, however, cutting headcount starts to look very attractive. And often the stock market responds favorably to such approaches, which simply tells us that although the market may choose, it does not necessarily, in specific instances, choose wisely.

Base pay looks good as a target for cutting for other reasons as well. Through annuitization it often grows independently from productivity. Meanwhile, a sense of entitlement is generated among workers. Both of these effects are problems for employers. Base pay is also problematic when the administration of pay is separate from other elements of compensation administration. Finally, resistance to change compounds the challenge of altering base pay.

Employers have tried three main ways of constructing pay: paying the job, paying the person, and paying the results. Each of these, and their variations, has its own problems, and none has resolved the fundamental issues associated with base pay.

Some innovations worth considering are broad-banding, variable pay, splitting the increase, and vertical and horizontal alignment. Implementing any or all of these will require both cultural change and structural change. Both require new thinking on the part of employers and employees. Although it is imperative to implement better approaches to base pay, change agents should be realistic and attempt the kinds of changes that suit the employer-employee mix. Any such effort can profit from a conscious inclusion of the five I's: ideas, input, involvement, information, and improvement.

The Augmentation Accelerant

The Push for Performance

The second term of the total compensation equation is augmented pay. Augmented pay is any compensation that is paid on a one-time basis, from overtime to commissions to stock options. By "one-time basis" I mean that there is no guarantee that the augmentation will be received again, though, of course, it may be paid on many separate occasions.

Augmented pay comes in three main forms: insourcing pay, profit sharing pay, and incentive pay. I refer to these types of pay as the *augmentation accelerant* because they provide immediate growth in pay and push performance faster.

■ **Types of Augmented Pay**

The first type of augmented pay, insourcing pay, is extra pay for extra work that is *insourced,* meaning that it is performed by employees over and above the duties for which they are normally paid. Overtime pay is a simple example. Some organizations use this method a lot, and some (as in "forced overtime") depend on it. It works best, however, when employees can choose it.

Insourcing is a real boon to the employer, because the firm gets an employee who is already trained and ready to go. Employers who have not considered insourcing as a regular policy would be well advised to do so, and to regularly publish a list of available extra work.

The second form of augmented pay is profit sharing. The word says it all: as organizations make more against budget or in terms of profit, they share some of that gain with employees on some preannounced basis (or, sometimes, an unannounced basis). Although the term is used for some specific kinds of distributions as well, I use it as a general term for the sharing of profits, either through cash or an equity stake. (I say "profits" because gainsharing usually relates to the bottom line, or at least to the expectation of certain bottom-line results.) At the CEO level, profit sharing may take the form of "options for stock." In the middle mass of workers, it may be called a profit sharing bonus. It provides an overall, rather than specific, connection of rewards to productivity behaviors, because there are many factors that affect profit that individual employees cannot influence.

I think, as do others, that such sharing of the profit gains is too constricted today, too concentrated within a top group of senior managers. The spread from lowest- to highest-paid workers is enormous. When those at the top cream off the gains, those remaining in the organization lose motivation and interest. Recall from Chapter One that Don Lowman makes that point; compensation guru Ed Lawler agrees. Lawler argues that companies should spread stock options throughout the workforce, rather than concentrate them on very senior executives. Only then can firms expect to retain key technology and leadership talent effectively. Only 15 percent to 20 percent of all U.S. corporations make most or all employees eligible for stock options. This number is far too low.[1]

Because firms are, in a sense, communities, it is appropriate that gains and pains be shared. Further, profit sharing can be part of a motivational package. After all, why should an employee work especially hard just so the owners can be rich? The plans of newer companies—technology companies like Microsoft, for example—illustrate this practice.

The flip side of profit sharing also applies. "Loss sharing" means that when bad times come, everyone takes a hit; we do not protect senior executives while laying off hundreds of regular Joes and Janes. As a practical matter, profit sharing and loss sharing mean that gains and losses are shared broadly, though not necessarily equally. Historically, senior management has been overrewarded in good times and overprotected in bad ones. This view is not just opinion; it is based on Deming's observation that the output of an organization is the output of a *system*.[2]

A good example of this philosophy in action is the Red Hot Law Group, founded by Evelyn Ashley: "Ever hear of a law firm that gives its clerical staff a stake in the company? This one does. Staff receive a portion of the accelerator-owned stock options as a bonus. 'Don't be a hog. Hogs get slaughtered,' advises Ashley. 'I wanted to create an equal, easygoing practice built on the premise that your name doesn't have to be on the wall to be considered an equal.'"[3]

There is room for lots of disagreement about profit sharing as a principle, and in terms of the specifics of any program. The point, however, is that as employers come to understand that quality and productivity are more the result of teams and networks than individuals, they need to share the wealth and the pain. Ours has been a "winner-take-all" society, as reflected in the title of a book by Robert Frank and Phil Cook: *The Winner-Take-All Society: Why the Few at the Top Get So Much More Than the Rest of Us.*[4] We need to move from "winner take all" to "winner take a lot but not all." Otherwise, "pay envy" will erode motivation and lower productivity, harming the bottom line.[5] Companies are moving this way. According to data from Hewitt Associates presented by Elizabeth Wing of *USA Today*, in 1996 21 percent of companies had equity sharing stock options plans; in 2000 that fraction moved to 50 percent.[6]

The third kind of augmented pay—and the one that will be the main focus of this chapter—is incentive pay, also termed *inducement pay* or *pay for performance* and sometimes *gainsharing.*[7] Incentive pay is the extra that workers get for achieving a specific objective or level of performance or by creating certain rather short-term gains (such as expenditure gains against budget). Today even teachers are getting on the bandwagon of incentive pay. Between 1991 and 1999, the fraction of employers that have moved to incorporate such plans rose from 15 percent to 42 percent.[8]

Incentive pay has become popular for a couple of reasons, both of which relate to productivity. First, employers have already done what they can to improve their bottom line through downsizing. As I noted in Chapter Three, downsizing is a "quick fix" because it can produce results quickly, but only once. Once you have downsized, that's about it, because you have few folks left to get rid of. Now employers are seeking to tweak the remaining workforce into more productivity by leveraging compensation, in whatever form, and aligning it with the performance of the individuals and the organization. There is a renewed interest in the sensible feeling that those who contribute more to the bottom line should see some of that contribution in their own bottom line. This reflects, of course, "Harberger's Differential," which I mentioned in Chapter Two. But Harberger reflects a base-pay orientation. It is meant to act as a motivational tool. Employers play "Let's Make a Deal." If you, the employee, do such-and-such, then your reward will be thus-and-so.

Second, employers are very interested—and rightly so—in getting their money's worth out of the payroll. And they sense—rightly again, I think—that there is room for improvement in their workforce, an unused capacity that, through a proper motivational system, could be energized. For example, many employees give themselves a raise by working less. A recent radio report suggests that smokers, to cite one group, take forty minutes a day in smoke breaks. In a company of a hundred smokers, working forty weeks a year (allowing for vacations, sick leaves, holidays, and so on), that is 13,333 hours a year up in smoke. At $20 per hour, that amounts to more than $260,000 in do-it-yourself raises.

To take another example, each term I ask my MBA students the following question: "Based on your experience, how much work actually goes on at work?" Only very rarely does the answer go above 80 percent of the week. The median answer is around 60 percent. This result is astonishing. If this informal sampling is in fact representative, then in the "best" firms, there is still a day a week of time available for mobilization. In the average company, that number jumps to two days. It seems that most employees are paid for their dissatisfaction rather than for their work.[9] A popular management analyst's anecdote says that somebody once asked Pope John XXIII how many people worked in the Vatican; he thought for a while and replied, "About half."

Employers, then, have good reasons to think that there is untapped productivity in their organizations, that there are more resources available to do work in the organization than are being utilized. Ed Lawler feels that an effective pay system can increase the motivation of individuals to perform by as much as 40 percent![10] Quotas and rates set by unions are only the tip of the hidden capacity iceberg.

Many employers feel that, with the proper inducements, this reserve can be tapped, and they use incentives to do it. There are typically two kinds of incentives, short-term incentives and long-term ones.[11] Short-term incentives are those that relate to a project or some specific, time-bound (daily, weekly, monthly) objective. These incentives should be paid at the completion of the goal; "Milk-Bones" is an appropriate metaphor. "Gainsharing" tends to work on a monthly basis, for example.

Long-term incentives are a bit more complicated, because they reflect three kinds of approaches and usage. Some long-term incentives are for long-term contributions; an "MVP" award is an example. This may be a substantial cash award to an employee for exceptional contribution over time. The second type of long-term incentive deals with long-term performance, as opposed to long-term contribution. Although there are occasions when this distinction is hard to make, the contribution approach looks to all-around value, while the performance approach looks to goal-based accomplishments. Here again, this may be a cash award based on the achievement of certain numbers for the total year, or for consistent high performance (for example, twelve consecutive months). The difference between this and a short-term performance incentive lies in the span of time over which the performance is measured. The difference between long-term incentives and profit sharing is that long-term incentives focus on individual performance, while profit is driven by corporate performance.

There is a third way in which companies use the concept of long-term incentives, although it has more to do with pay administration than with incentives for performance. It is an approach that seeks to bind the worker to the organization by paying the incentive dollars over time. Incentives—either short-term or long-term, in our previous usage—are distributed over time, on a "some now, some later" basis. Using this approach, the firm might promise a "short-term incentive" of $10,000, but pay only half this year. The other half it keeps for next year, and mixes in with half of whatever additional incentive is due then. (This is a place where short-term incentives merge with, or become, longer-term ones.)[12] Or, with options of one sort or another, employees cannot exercise the options until some specified time.

On the surface, incentive pay seems to reflect a straightforward deal: "We pay extra, and you produce extra." The Lincoln Electric Company in Cleveland has used this approach successfully for years in the United States, though it did not work as well in Europe. (Admittedly, this is an extreme example.)[13] But it does not always work, even here. Why not? Paradoxically, it might well be that incentive pay actually works to undermine performance rather than enhance it. Indeed, it turns out that there are a number of problems in providing incentive pay.

■ The Problems

Although incentive pay always seems like a good way to motivate people, it can backfire. Sometimes it is given to performers and nonperformers alike. At other times it is given for reasons extraneous to job performance.

There are other drawbacks as well. Here we'll explore eleven of them, which I characterize as follows:

- Folly
- Misapplied or overcredited individualism; pay envy
- Punishment effects and destruction of intrinsic motivation
- Poor performance appraisal
- Greed: owners covet the gains

□

- The "who benefits?" dilemma: using percent or dollar increases
- Lack of incentive for the haves
- Uncertainty
- Poor administration
- Calibration and customization
- Inappropriate control

I realize that eleven problems are a lot to keep straight. And perhaps they could have been combined in a shorter list. However, I saw no straightforward way to compress the list, so I am going with the full eleven. Suggested solutions—in the problems/solutions format, follow in another set of eleven. I think the larger number of problems here stems from the intellectual and theoretical complexities of the incentives idea, and the many hopes and perils it contains.

1. Folly

The first problem with incentive pay is folly, or, as Steve Kerr puts it, "rewarding A while hoping for B."[14] Kerr first published the book with this title in 1978. In 1996 it was reprinted as a "classic"—apparently, not much progress had been made!

Firms commit folly when they misspecify their purpose for incentive pay. As I mentioned earlier, too often we hope for productivity but reward time; we hope for results but reward longevity; we want workers to be committed, yet we pay CEOs four hundred times what the average worker makes. The problem for many companies is that they actually get what they reward.

Kerr mentions some elements that drive folly that are worth noting here: overfascination with objective criteria, overfascination with highly visible behaviors, overemphasis on pleasing (lying and hypocrisy), and overemphasis on morality and equity rather than efficiency (and, I might add, effectiveness).[15]

2. Misapplied or Overcredited Individualism: Pay Envy

A second problem is misapplied individualism, or failing, as W. Edwards Deming argues, to understand that the system, rather than individuals, produces much of what we call "results." American society is highly individualistic. The kind of explanation we look for is better exemplified by the mountain man than by the wagon train. But in real life, results are more often produced by the wagon train—that is, the team. Lots of great individual players do not an orchestra or a team make.

We know this, yet we forget it. The World War II acronym SNAFU (situation normal, all f _ _ _ ed up) was a tacit recognition of the effects of systems. Deming's work on the production of quality clearly reveals this system effect. He distinguishes between "common causes of variation" and "individual causes of variation." According to Deming, common causes of variation— whether good variations or bad ones (profits or losses)—are more important than individual ones. Rewarding individuals for system results makes incentive pay look random, because, in terms of root causes, it *is* random. The same applies on the other side of the equation: firms often overpunish individuals for systemic problems and issues.[16]

There is another problem with overcrediting individuals. Sometimes the incentives awarded to individuals in a system or team are so great that they destroy the motivation of others. In "Listen Up, Managers: Fat Paychecks Don't Always Guarantee Success," the *Wall Street Journal*'s Gordon Fairclough cautions that doing more for the "few" can irritate the "many," causing "pay envy."[17]

3. Punishment Effects and Destruction of Intrinsic Motivation

A third problem is that, perversely, incentive pay can have real-world effects directly opposite to its intent. Analyst Alfi Kohn has made this point in a book called *Punished by Rewards* and in a spate of articles.[18]

Incentive pay can punish in several ways. First, incentive rewards harm the motivation of those who do not receive them (pay envy). Hence their usefulness is perhaps more limited than one might think. Additionally, rewards have a tendency to *efface,* or lose their value. Hence the amount of the reward often must keep going up. Then there is the problem of comparisons. While rewards have intrinsic value ($1,000 is, after all, $1,000), it sometimes matters what others get. If everyone gets $1,000, then at least the psychological value of the reward may be decreased, since for incentive pay to be motivational it presumably has to be somewhat rare.

Second, once the system is set up for giving incentive rewards, it is usually a few who get them repeatedly. This truth we all remember from getting gold stars in first and second grade. It was always a guy named Charlie H. who just edged me out!

But there is more. Incentive pay can punish the system as well, by creating an organization where people work only for the incentives. When that happens, incentive pay effectively destroys intrinsic motivation. All of us who have struggled with the question of incentive pay for our kids recognize this problem. Should we pay kids for chores? On one hand, we want to give them a little something in recognition of their efforts. On the other hand, we feel that, as family members, they should chip in as a matter of felt obligation. Then there is the problem of price. I once offered my son some money for cutting the grass. He conferred with his friends and came back with a revised pricing proposal, including so much for the actual cutting, so much for bagging, so much for clipping, and so on. Then, after further consideration—and while I was still reviewing the proposal in front of me—he raised his prices by 20 percent! The "What's in it for me?" mind-set is not a fundamentally good one for the organization for several reasons, not the least of which is that the price keeps going up.

4. Poor Performance Appraisal

We tend to think of performance appraisal as associated with the raise that is associated with base pay. And indeed it often is. I have located it here, rather than in the preceding chapter, because augmented pay—and incentive pay in particular—is really about metrics and measures attached to reward dollars. If incentive pay is going to work at all, then it needs to be connected to concrete accomplishments—which in turn are connected to various cash rewards: incentives, or gainsharing amounts, or bonuses. The key to linking these elements is performance appraisal. Hence, the fourth problem is poor performance appraisal systems. There are really two problems in performance appraisal. One is specifying the goals to be achieved. To some extent, the problem of specifying appropriate goals for individuals and systems was something I already discussed in the first problem, folly. Having achieved goals description, however, still leaves open the problem of creating metrics for them and a process of providing feedback and evaluation to employees so that they can better achieve the goals. It's not enough to specify goals; managers need to help individuals, through feedback and evaluation, *get* to the goal. (And that means holding the goal steady and resisting the temptation to make it a moving target!) If appropriate metrics are not developed at the front end, the discussion often turns on how the employees are assessed, rather than what the employees did.[19] This point is relevant both to issues of base pay, including some of its newer variants, and to incentive pay. I have placed it here because of its special relationship to "stretch" goals of the sort that incentive pay is designed to encourage and reward.

Effective feedback is rare in organizations today. This problem has historical roots. In pay-the-job systems the job was, well, the job. You did it or not. There was no sense in which your employer helped you do it—that would have sounded stupid to all concerned! Goals were attached to the job, and were often outlined as procedures rather than accomplishments. Hence managers did not have to give feedback, and little organizational experience developed around it. Add to this problem the general difficulty of "giving bad news," which is how appraisals are generally seen, and one can understand why there is limited enthusiasm and much avoidance and defensiveness surrounding them. The typical evaluation is often called the "vanishing appraisal" because the boss starts to give the appraisal, and then drifts into a discussion of football or some other irrelevancy. Someone at one of the auto companies told me he got his "performance appraisal" from the adjoining stall in the men's room, when a voice floated over saying something like, "You have done a great job this year, Jim. I'm putting you in for a 15 percent bonus!" It is hard to know how to respond to a thing like that.

Another part of the problem is that the climate of performance appraisal is almost always negative: "Here is what you did wrong (or at least not well enough)." This atmosphere is, naturally, a stress on giver and receiver alike. While it is not rocket science to think that employees might also like to know what they did right so they can continue doing it, too often that kind of feedback, if it is given at all, is swamped by the criticisms. Hence the negativity cycle.

Apart from these general issues, there are a number of specific other problems and errors that are so common they deserve to be mentioned here:

- *Halo or horns error:* Looking at the person's reputation rather than specific behaviors
- *Primacy error:* Being unwilling to reevaluate a first impression in the light of new information
- *Recency error:* Paying overmuch attention to events in the recent past

- *Leniency and severity errors:* Working too much on one side of the curve or the other
- *Central tendency:* Tending to lump everyone around the mean
- *Clone error:* Being especially positive to employees who are like oneself
- *Spillover:* Paying too much attention to the results of prior ratings as an influence on the current one

Of course, none of us actually commit any of these obvious mistakes. Yet each of us has experienced some or all of them. I wonder how that happens?

5. Greed: Owners Covet the Gains

The fifth problem can undermine the effort to institute incentive pay. As I mentioned in earlier chapters, owners and bosses commonly still believe that paying employees less is good. That is the employee-as-cost model. The problem with this model is that it is silent on results, ignoring the underlying truth that employees are investments, and if well compensated they can create extraordinary value. Part of the idea of incentive pay is to affirm that people will share in various ways in the value they create. Indeed, the idea of "investment" can be thought of as a way of talking about firm risk management—making sure that the return on your "employee investment" is as good as your return on other investments.[20]

The problem is that, when that value begins to be created, owners and managers want it; I have seen lots of cases of this "clawback" approach. It's a kind of greed, but one that is nourished by misapplied individualism. Managers think somehow *they* did it, and are thus *entitled* to the extra value. If in the process ordinary employees are left out, well, that's the way it is in our winner-take-all society.[21]

6. The "Who Benefits" Dilemma: Using Percent or Dollar Increases

If firms do pay out incentives, they must decide how to do it. One of the big questions is whether to use proportions of base (thus giving more dollars to those with higher bases) or cash (thus giving a higher percentage of base to those with lower bases). One may say, "Well, each employee is entitled to a percentage of the gains, based on regular salary." Those with higher salaries like this approach, of course, and consider it just. Take a 10 percent distribution. The highly paid manager making $100,000 gets $10,000 in incentive pay, while the lowly assistant making $20,000 gets $2,000. The rich get richer, the poor get seriously annoyed. So we move to dollars. Let's say everyone gets $5,000. That means that the assistant making $20,000 gets a 25 percent bump, while the manager making $100,000 gets a 5 percent bump. Same dollars, different percentages. Either way there is kvetching.

7. Lack of Incentive for the Haves

Incentive pay, of course, works only if people need or can use the reward, and not everyone can do so—call it the "executive pay" problem. It crops up when people have no conventional use for their incentive pay; the value becomes only symbolic. At the top level, with incentive pay in the neighborhood of hundreds of millions of dollars—and in the first part of 2000 two executives went over a billion, for one year—one needs to ask whether incentive pay deserves the name. I am not raising here the issue of whether such bonus amounts are proper or ethical. I am only asking the question of how you motivate a sated dog. The problem doesn't come up just at Olympian heights of pay, either. At levels well below a billion dollars, many people find that their needs and priorities are such that after a certain point extra money is simply not a great motivator.

8. Uncertainty

The next problem is the inherent uncertainty of incentive pay, a problem made worse because of the system effect discussed earlier. Many times employees simply cannot control what they would need to control to make sure they get the reward. Apart from this, uncertainty is inherent in the very notion of incentive pay. For some people, uncertainty is an added reward: these are the individuals who thrive on risk and can take the inevitable downsides as well as enjoy the upsides. On the other hand, the more typical worker with a spouse and family may not feel quite the same way. Hence the possibility of bigger gains, associated with the possibility of bigger losses, may not serve as a motivational tool for some, or for some at some life points.

Of course, the uncertainty of incentive pay has other elements as well. For example, options granted as part of a reward system may become more costly than the stock itself. Some corporations reprice incentives to take market changes into account. So there is uncertainty too, at the very top of the reward system.

9. Poor Administration

Incentive pay may be problematic in ways that have nothing to do with the specific incentives. A good idea, badly implemented, becomes a bad idea—and incentive programs are often poorly administered. Incentive programs need to give the right incentive, the right way, the first time. When the rubber hits the road, program administrators need to deliver.

Lawler discusses some of the elements of a good system in his book *Pay and Organizational Development*.[22] He argues that satisfaction with pay elements such as incentive pay is a function of several factors:

- *How much is received.* The amount of the reward often, though not always, matters. Americans are big on big.

- *How much others are perceived to receive.* This is the fairness doctrine. Incentives, regardless of whether they are candy bars or bundles of bucks, should be fair. Fair means proportional. Whether one is rewarding effort or results, incentives need to be proportional across recipients. The following equations capture the principle:

$$\text{My reward / my input (effort)} = \text{your reward / your input (effort)}$$

$$\text{My reward / my output (results)} = \text{your reward / your output (results)}$$

- *The identity of the "others."* If the "others" who receive incentive pay are perceived, within the firm's subculture, to deserve it, that is probably OK. If, on the other hand, the deserving and the undeserving alike get so-called incentive pay, that is poor administration.
- *Perceptions about what should be received.* Part of the "should" here is the fairness doctrine. But another part is the appropriateness doctrine. Incentives that seem minuscule compared to the firm's profits seem more like an insult than a reward—another way that employees can be punished by incentive pay.
- *How recipients are selected.* In many cases, firms use seemingly arbitrary selection procedures. Indeed, the criteria are often unknown to the employees. Hence the reward might better be called a "surprise." This point connects to the one about the identity of the others who receive awards. For incentive pay to work, the recipients need to be the right recipients, not the liars and the ingratiators.
- *Scarcity.* Incentives seem to work better if they are relatively rare. However, as I noted earlier, that defeats the purpose of motivating everyone (or at least giving everyone the opportunity to be motivated). Besides, does my $5,000 lose value be-

cause many others get the same amount? Well, yes, in a status sense, but no, in the sense that it's still $5,000. "Status inflation" is a real consideration, however. In the words of Gilbert (more or less), "When everybody's somebody, then nobody's anybody." That is one of the problems with incentives. There is an absolute value and a relative one. Status inflation occurs when rewards become too widespread.

- *Degree of visibility.* Incentive pay needs to be in the public domain. Some organizations have secret incentive pay: "Here is $20,000, but don't tell anyone." Again, the issue of status comes into play. The social value of an incentive is hugely diminished if it is private. Further, any motivational value that others might derive from it is gone.

10. Calibration and Customization

The next problem concerns the calibration of incentives. Calibration refers to getting the incentive "just right." Giving a dog more than it can actually eat only makes it sick. Giving it less than it needs does the same. Similarly, pay too little in the way of an incentive, and it becomes an irritant. Too much is over-compensation; employers do not get anything back for the extra dollars, and can even move into the disincentive region.

The term *honorarium* is designed to manage this expectation up front. Specifically, an honorarium is a cash gift that is presented in recognition of—but not as compensation for—something an employee has done. If I announce that an employee will get an honorarium of, say, $100 for something, I am specifically also saying that I am not paying the person the value of the contribution. This management of expectations tends to minimize irritation.

A "just right" incentive meets the test of proportionality; that is, the incentive is proportional to the contribution. "Just right" is based both on market conditions and on the employee. I may pay more for a famous consultant than for a less famous one; that proportionality is OK. By the same token, I may pay a great chef more than a good chef, a fabulous conductor more than a regular one, a great Samaritan more than a good Samaritan, a great finish carpenter more than a good one. Overcompensating—paying more than a contribution is worth—does not elicit any more effort than offering a proportional reward. It is money lost, and it raises a question, in the employee's mind, about whether the firm knows what it is doing. As with instant coffee, laundry detergent, and drinks, more is not always better.

Amount is one thing to consider when thinking about detergent; which detergent to use is also an issue. It depends on the clothes—and the washer. The same is true for compensation programs. Having the right amount of incentive, in the right package, is crucial.

11. Inappropriate Control

Finally, there is the problem of using incentives as a control device, taking the freedom away from subordinates to define and perform the work as they think best. Sometimes employers (and parents) use incentives to shape behavior in ways that *only* they wish, thus robbing the employee or offspring of freedom. Unless goals are shared, incentives become odious. Monica Langly talks about this in a lead *Wall Street Journal* article titled "The House, the Money—It'll All Be Yours; There's Just One Thing."[23] Her discussion of "family incentive plans" explores the ways that rich parents get their kids to do what they want—for example, "We'll pay you if your wife does not work." Resentment builds.

■ Suggested Solutions

Properly handled, incentive pay can be a key ingredient in a total compensation program. Let me begin this discussion of suggested solutions with some general observations on incentive pay and augmented pay programs, and then deal specifically with the problems I have mentioned.

An incentive pay program is a program to increase motivation to reach specific goals. To be successful, the program needs to accomplish two sets of things: do right, and do not do wrong. As simple as that sounds, this formulation contains a profound truth. Many people feel that, if they are doing right, they are not doing wrong. *Wrong.* You can be doing right and wrong at the same time because they are not the same things. A great sales rep can move a lot of product (doing right) and also run up outrageous expenses (doing wrong). Hence it is necessary to consciously emphasize doing the good and avoiding the bad. That is what excellence is, really. This discussion will attend to both.

To begin with, pay systems, including incentive programs, have to be workable in the firm setting. Part of being workable is being believable. They have to have face validity and "seem right." Another way of putting this point might be to ask, Can the average employee understand it? If the incentives program does not have the power of simplicity, it will not work, or at best will not work well.

Employees also need to have a line of sight between their own behaviors and the system goals on which the incentives are predicated. That is, if there is a goal whose achievement will bring reward, can the prospective recipient actually influence it? That is why profit sharing is not a good reward. Although I have argued that it is appropriate for other reasons to share the wealth, gainsharing does not *reward* because the overall gain is not, ordinarily, something individual employees can influence in ways they can understand.

And the program has to be trustworthy. Employees need to believe that the incentives will be paid, and experience must validate that belief.

Incentives work better if they are received close to the event, rather than, say, on an annual basis. Smaller, more connected incentive payments seem to work more effectively than larger, unconnected ones. Not that many of us would turn down a wad of cash, but without a connection to a specific achievement, an incentive is not a reward any more than winning the lottery is. Luck is good; a reward it is not.

In addition, incentives should be structured in such a way that employees remember them, and remember them as connected to achievements. This, of course, relates to the point about the way in which someone actually gets the reward. If the connection is missing, the value of the so-called reward as an incentive is completely lost.

There is a hierarchy of pay, based loosely on Maslow's hierarchy of needs. The most basic form of pay (base pay) deals with issues of regularity and security. We all need some of that. But once we move past this fundamental level to the notion of rewards, pay needs to be more customized and variegated, as needs are more unique and differentiated. Hence a one-size-fits-all reward system may not work. Up the ladder, as it were, incentive pay needs to become more diverse, more complex, more differentiated. As Lawler notes, "Incentive Pay systems seem to have more influence on motivation than they have on the importance attached to specific Incentive Pay."[24] This is because *motivation* is more within the control of the expectancies of the individual, while the value of specific incentives—liking money, for example—is heavily influenced by family, culture, and so on.

With these general ideas in hand, let's consider some solutions and general suggestions for the eleven problems detailed in the preceding section. Of course, complete solutions to all these complex problems cannot be fully detailed here. What follows are ideas and guidelines that can be considered in the context of adopting the total compensation approach advocated in this book.

1. Folly

To avoid paying for A while hoping for B, employers need to specify exactly what it is they want in return for augmented pay, and what they want to achieve with the program. What *are* the results for which you wish to pay? Do they meet the criteria specified in preceding sections?

In evaluating an incentive pay program, consider whether or not the problem of rewarding the wrong things affects you. Ask yourself—and ask employees—whether the program is specific enough to be useful. When you specify goals, they should be moderately difficult. Too easy, and they become a joke; too difficult, and they become a joke.

You may be familiar with two mnemonics for effective goal setting:

SMART Goals
Specific
Manageable
Achievable
Realistic
Timebound

SUCCESS Goals
Simple
Understandable
Competence-driven
Communicated clearly
Equitable
Share vision
Sustain enthusiasm

2. Misapplied or Overcredited Individualism: Pay Envy

Consider whether your firm is overemphasizing individuals at the cost of the team and the system. Be aware that individual talent does not a team or an orchestra make. A mix of individual and team incentive pay can make an effective package. That is on the upside. On the downside, be aware that the "messenger" of poor quality is only delivering what the system permits. Also consider complementing incentive pay for individual excellence (and punishments for individual failures) with profit sharing approaches to deal with team and system productivity.

3. Punishment Effects and Destruction of Intrinsic Motivation

Several suggestions apply here. First, try to keep base pay appropriate so that people will not have to work for incentive pay just to put food on the table. This is the problem with the "car sales" or total commission approach. When incentive pay is your only source of salary or base pay rather than coming as augmented pay, intrinsic motivation is destroyed. This point does not imply that base pay has to be high. Rather, looking at Norman Harberger's three levels (top 20 percent, at 15 percent above market; middle 60 percent, at market, more or less; and lowest 20 percent, at 15 percent or more below market), you can pay in a fairly narrow range, as long as you keep adjusting to reflect the actual market. (You do not have to be as careful about the bottom 20 percent!) Some employers are talking with me about how much they have to pay new hires. What they do not understand is that, yes, you usually pay more for new hires but when the gap between new hires and more senior employees gets large, it tells me that a company is exploiting its current hires by a "slow to market" strategy.

With respect to incentive pay specifically, ask yourself whether your firm might be overrewarding some employees. Keep in mind that incentives need to be complemented by programs designed to increase intrinsic motivation. Among the best of these are recognition and appreciation programs.

4. Poor Performance Appraisal

This area is one that is generally so bad that anything you try will be an improvement. Train managers to provide solid, state-of-the-art performance appraisals.

Good performance appraisal starts with well-specified goals (though, as emphasized earlier, it goes well beyond that).

Once the goals are in place, managers should provide both feedback and evaluation—and not just once a year. Feedback should be

- Ongoing
- Frequent
- Issue oriented (focused on performance to be corrected or praised)
- Nonjudgmental
- Inclusive of both strengths and weaknesses
- Sufficiently detailed so that the receiver understands it
- Geared to the style of the receiver
- Two way
- Owned by the giver (no "'They' say this and that")
- Focused on those things the person can control
- Given in appropriate amounts (no "dumping")

Lots of feedback builds the case for evaluation. Evaluation differs from feedback in that it

- Adds the notion of judgment
- Is fateful—it affects your life!
- Involves the element of power
- Involves the elements of working to standard
- Is usually the most poorly handled part of the performance appraisal process

Successful evaluation uses both the goals with which the process was begun and the information gained from the feedback sessions. Evaluation is results-oriented, while feedback is more process-oriented. The results were part of the goal set. Hence the employee knows the standards that are being used from the beginning.

In doing feedback and evaluation work, managers should deploy both coaching and counseling skills. Managers coach when they provide information, explain procedures, set standards, or provide instruction from their experience. Coaching is appropriate for problems of information, as when people do not know how to operate a new word-processing program and simply need to learn how to work it. There is no attitude problem; they are not resisting it, they just need the information, or understanding. In some cases the employee has been misplaced in terms of ability.

Counseling, in contrast, is emotional work. It is needed when an attitude problem prevents the employee from absorbing coaching information. Counseling needs to come before coaching, because if there is an attitude block, then the employee is unable to process the helpful resources. The block can be something specific ("I hate computers") or something more general ("I am worried about my low level of technological capability"). Employers, of course, cannot deal with all the kinds of attitude problems, but some degree of listening, validating, encouraging, probing, asking for answers, and supporting (the feeling, not the action) can go a long way toward creating a new, more accepting attitude into which coaching skills can then be brought.

5. Greed: Owners Covet the Gains

If you're in a position to covet the gains, the suggestion is simple: don't. Easier said, of course, than done. Or, if you do, handle your temptation the way Jimmy Carter handled adultery: covet only in your heart, and pay out. The problem is that once employees see a "clawback" process occurring, trust is lost. Once lost, it can almost never be regained.

If you're not one of the lucky ones in a position to covet rather than be coveted against, there is no good answer. You may get sandbagged by owners clawing back the promised gains. The best you can do here is be prepared for selfishness.

6. The "Who Benefits" Dilemma: Using Percent or Dollar Increases

This problem is something of a no-win, as the word *dilemma* implies. One possible solution is to split the reward (and the gain-sharing also) between dollars and proportions. Half and half is a good start. Publicly recognizing the downsides of whatever pick is made, instead of demeaning the people who point out those downsides, will help. There really is no well-established way to deal with this dilemma; local knowledge and practice is a good guide if half and half does not seem workable.

7. Lack of Incentive for the Haves

Recognize that there are people for whom money does not function as a strong incentive. Ed Lawler puts it this way: "There is no evidence that very large stock-option grants have a positive effect either on corporate performance or executive motivation. At some point additional amounts of incentives simply lose their power to motivate, essentially because individuals are already at their maximum motivation levels."[25]

And those people are not always dot-com trillionaires, either. Some of them are people who seek and have found a simpler life. Others are older people who want more leisure and less wealth hassle. Then there are those for whom psychic income and quality of life mean more than additional money. That is really the central point of the total compensation approach: find out what people want. Those who do not want money usually have something else that is of interest. Find it; offer it. (Here again, recognition and appreciation programs can be part of the solution.)

□

8. Uncertainty

Recognize that the uncertainty of incentive pay is an attraction to some and a stress to others. Point out the upsides *and* the downsides. Do not pretend that there are no downsides. Uncertainty is what risk really is; people often overemphasize the potential benefits and underemphasize the potential hazards. Working with cafeteria compensation allows employees to choose, to a degree, a level of risk that they themselves feel works for them.

9. Poor Administration

Poor administration is, of course, the sum total of many of the things discussed in the chapter. To be fair, much "poor administration" is simply nonadministration. Somehow, somewhere, rules were set for reasons that no one remembers, and people have continued to mindlessly implement them ever since. That is what Robert Merton has called "means ritualism." As noted in Chapter One, means ritualism refers to that situation in which the goals have been forgotten, but the programmed means continue to operate like some outdated computer code that will not go away.

Several points about administration should be kept in mind. To begin with, *do* administer, that is, manage, in the best sense of those terms. Think about the augmented pay program. Use it thoughtfully. Change it regularly. Ask employees to help in developing and changing it; few things are worse than another "flavor of the month" issuing solely from Human Resources.

Scan the environment for best practices. Try some of your own. Experiment. Do not be afraid to try some things out. Do them small at first, and capitalize on "success through small wins."

Remember Occam's Razor? William of Occam was a four-teenth-century bishop who devised a test for evaluating competing mathematical proofs that bears his name to this day. Of two proofs, the one with the fewest steps wins. The principle really means that simpler is better. Always. But simple plans are not simplistic ones. Simple plans do the fundamental job (and solve the equation). Simplistic plans look good—and fail quickly.

Do keep measures, and look at the pattern by employee, from year to year. Observe trends by person and by department. Employees, teams, divisions should be improving. Individuals and units that show negative trends—and trends are important—should be considered further. I stress the importance of trends because anyone may have a bad measure one quarter, one year, one whenever. The point is much more in the trend than in the instance.

A second thing to consider is the presence of soft spots—areas of negativity or weakness concealed within an overall wonderful performance. Recall the definition of excellence: doing good and avoiding bad. Here is a place where it specifically applies. The spectacular sales rep with outrageous expenses (or a proclivity for some other problem performance area) needs to have these bad elements addressed. Employers all too often let stars get away with lots of stuff in part because the employees are stars, but also because the employers do not trace performance. Even at the University of Michigan, the world center for data collection and data analysis, we are poor in this area. Every faculty member is rated on every course. The material we receive each year, however, refers only to the courses for that year; if we want to see any trends we need to calculate them ourselves. Trend lines and overall data are generally absent.

Using some of the suggestions and observations offered here and elsewhere, you can develop a state-of-the-art compensation system. This involves not only structure (having the right parts) but process (change). Process improvements mean both updating and customizing. They also mean having the right people at the interface of the employee and the organization—that is, people who take pride in their compensation work.

Finally, as I say in other contexts, communication is key. Solid communication helps you get more bang for your buck.[26]

10. Calibration and Customization

Calibration means finding the right incentive, or combination of incentives, to hit the mark. This is where the firm needs to create the menu from which the workers choose. In some cases it might be the payout of a percentage of sales or profits. In other cases it might be a dinner for the employee and a partner or spouse, or a trip. The point is to continue to be sensitive to this issue, and provide the gift of "enoughness"—not "too littleness" or "too much of a muchness."

To achieve this targeting, you need to do a couple of things. The first is to develop a pay policy—deciding as a firm what level of compensation your enterprise can make available. Nonprofits, for example, will not have the level of pay that for-profits usually have. They need to compete on other grounds. But making this decision, explicating it and explaining it, is a crucial first step. It is important for firms to be able to feel good about what they can do rather than bad about what they cannot do.

Within the context of the policy, it is vital to keep asking employees—or, more precisely, opinion leaders within the employee group—about the incentive fit.

Robert Green looks at this issue in the context of the type of worker and the various "risk packages" that various types of workers might find appealing. His augmented and variable pay suggestions are presented in Table 4.1. Green also has a form of compensation he calls "ownership." It is useful to think about here because, although it is actually a form of augmented pay, it is pay *in a form* that binds the worker to the fate of the organization more closely than simple cash. In terms of calibration, it is important to consider the different psychological effects of cash rewards and ownership rewards.

Table 4.1. Augmented Pay Packages Customized by Type of Worker

Compensation Element	Type of Worker			
	Career Professional	Project Professional	Career Worker	Contract Worker
Augmented pay (variable pay)	Profit sharing Project incentives	Project incentives Venture participation (cash)	Profit sharing Performance sharing Individual productivity incentives	Individual productivity incentives Project incentives
Ownership	Employee stock ownership plans (ESOP) Stock options Profit sharing in company stock	Venture participation (equity)	Employee stock ownership plans (ESOP) Stock options Profit sharing in company stock	None

Source: Robert Green, "The Impact of Occupational Culture on Rewards Strategy," *ACA Journal 8*, no. 3 (Third Quarter, 1999): 13.

Table 4.1 also provides a column for contract workers. Typically they are not thought about in the compensation equation, in part because they are not your employees in the usual sense, and also because they sometimes cost a good bit more than regular workers doing the same job. In nursing homes, for example, "pool" nurses are considerably more expensive than "employee" nurses. Hence employers are reluctant to provide rewards for contract workers on top of the basic price. I think it is useful to keep them in mind, however, if only because they are working on your behalf, if not "for" you. Their motivation and orientation are important to consider across the board.

Of course these suggestions are just that; in cafeteria compensation workers get to package things themselves a bit. Is Green right? I am not sure. But I am sure he is on the right track.

11. Inappropriate Control

The suggestion here is a simple one. Employers need to develop shared goals with employees. Otherwise what looks like an incentive to you looks like a big stick to them. Employers, like parents, have preferences—charities they like, political parties they like, social attitudes they like. It is tempting to apply that skewed version of golden rule here—the one who has the gold makes the rules—and use augmented pay, or access to augmented pay opportunities, as a way to further these nonbusiness preferences. Obviously—I say *obviously* but, obviously, it is not obvious to some—this use of augmented pay is to be avoided. The business of business is business. Or, in the famous phrase of Stephen Covey, "The main thing is to keep the main thing the main thing." Augmented pay is best used to enhance business success—and employee success is both a precursor and a result of business success. To begin to broaden its use to further other goals dilutes and ultimately vitiates its central purpose.

■ Concluding Suggestions

Beyond the specific suggestions just offered, firms should keep in mind that all incentive pay effaces over time. By that I mean rewards wear out. What motivated someone yesterday does not always do it today. There are a couple of kinds of wearing away to keep in mind. One is that there is a tendency for the price to go up. My son, who has been mowing the grass for five bucks, is now angling for ten—with benefits and a sign-on bonus! Employers roundly blame employees for this "greedy and grabby" posture. Sometimes, of course, that is right. Often, though, it is because the employer was not keeping up with the market. (My son talked to other kids and saw he was being undercompensated!) Hence the other side of "rising price" is "rising market." Employers need to keep an eye on the market and adjust accordingly.

The second kind of wearing away occurs when the specific incentive loses meaning. This can occur as employees change (a fat bonus may not mean all that much to a fifty-something fat— or just chubby—cat) or because certain incentives simply lose their luster (*another* dinner at the Four Seasons . . .).

For this reason a good incentive pay system needs to be continually revisited, reviewed, and reinvented. New challenges need to be put in place. New skills have to be provided and taught. In short, an incentive pay system is a dynamic system— one that needs to be constantly upgraded, adjusted, and customized. Many firms want the benefits of incentive pay without the work. It can't be done.

CHAPTER SUMMARY

Augmented pay involves three kinds of *overpay,* or pay beyond salary: insourcing, profit sharing, and incentive pay. Insourcing is useful, and employers may want to look at developing it into an organized program. Profit sharing is a global sharing of profit. While it does not function effectively as a reward, there are other reasons (such as fairness) to move in this direction, reasons that are basically social and organizational. The social ones are important because we do not want, as a society, to have lots of people with really low pay. After all, as Henry Ford pointed out when he raised the daily wage to five bucks on the grounds that he wanted his employees to make enough to buy his cars, a consumer economy depends on consumers with reasonable spending power. The organizational reasons relate back to our overindividualistic society. We prefer the mountain man to the wagon train. Yet as Deming and the quality people have pointed out, sustained firm wealth is really much more of a collective product than we like to admit. And if the augmented pay comes in the form of ownership elements (equity rewards) it may interest employees more in seeking to influence the fate of the company in a positive way.

Incentive pay, one of the hottest topics today, is extra, one-time pay for achieving specific targets or goals. Incentive pay can work well if properly handled, with clear goals, clear line of sight, payment close to the event, and so on. Still, there are a number of problems with incentive pay. Some have easily articulated solutions; some don't.

Augmented pay, whether in the form of insourcing, profit sharing, an incentive pay program, or some combination of these, can be a valuable part of the total compensation array of tools. Like all tools, augmented pay requires work and skill in application. Throwing money at employees without pausing to find out if the money will do the job does no more good than throwing money at any other problem.

Indirect Pay

The Befuddlement of Benefits

The third term in the total compensation equation is indirect pay, more popularly known as *benefits*.[1] One can think of benefits as that part of the total compensation package, other than pay for time worked, that is paid for mainly or entirely by the employer.[2] Begun during World War II when wage and price controls were in effect, benefits have risen over the years. They meet several kinds of compensation needs.

First, benefits are a way—a delivery vehicle as it were—of paying part of the compensation on different terms from base pay. There may be a value in paying in this different way. I will discuss this potential in a moment. There is also some tax deferral advantage to paying compensation through benefits.

Second, benefits are a way of providing protection against inevitable life events such as retirement, and possible life events such as illness. While extreme free-market thinkers would argue for "each tub on its own bottom" (or each employee . . .), even the most hardened advocate hates to see people slipping off their lily pad into the muck. If base pay and augmented pay are the "money now" part of Schelling's discussion (recall "ego-nomics" from Chapter One), then benefits are "money later."

Third, benefits are a way of leveraging the buying power of employers so as to get things employees need or want at lower prices: glasses, health and life insurance, mortgages, and so on.

Some benefits, of course, are legally mandated, such as workers' compensation, unemployment compensation, and Social Security. The more interesting type of benefits for our purposes, and the ones that are the subject of this chapter, are those that are *employer*-elective, such as health insurance and employer-funded retirement plans. Let's begin the discussion with a question so basic it may seem strange to ask it: Why do companies shoulder the cost of this kind of compensation in the first place?

■ Why Do Companies Pay Benefits?

One might argue that benefits only involve the employer in end-less administrative hassles and arguments that any company would be better off without. And many would agree with this assessment. As one CEO put it, "Benefits—don't get me started. We are spending a bucketload of money on them, the bills keep coming, they don't do a damn thing for us, and they are a con-stant source of headaches." Nonetheless, there are three driving values or philosophies that push employers into the benefits game: the compensation philosophy, the social insurance philosophy, and the "employees want them" (or "keeping up with the competition") philosophy.

The Compensation Philosophy

For some, benefits are simply compensation delivered in another form. This method of delivering compensation developed in part simply as a matter of opportunity. When wages were frozen during the World War II era, increases in compensation had to be given some other way. Then there are the economies of scale. In some cases, employers can provide a value to employees at a much reduced cost, relative to the salary demands that would result if employees had to provide that same value for themselves. Medical costs are a good example.

The Social Insurance Philosophy

Benefits are also a response to certain social welfare concerns.[3] America has chosen to provide many of its social programs through the workplace. Medical and disability insurance, workers' compensation, and unemployment compensation are examples. In many of these programs, employers are "partnered" with government. Retirement, for example, is provided for most Americans through Social Security, but organizations—as well as employees—must pay into the Social Security Trust Fund (that is, they pay FICA—Federal Insurance Contribution Act—taxes with their federal income tax returns). Many firms, and most large ones that offer benefits, have a program that supplements Social Security.

Benefits are also a way to provide more equal compensation. The variance of the value of benefits is less than the variance for wages. If salaries and wages are, relatively speaking, more achievement-based, then benefits are, relatively speaking, more need- or equality-based.

The "Employees Want Them" Philosophy

Expectations are powerful producers of behavior. The fact that so many organizations have benefits and that they have become a part of the social fabric means that most firms are hard put not to offer them. To be sure, some firms are offering temporary or part-time positions without benefits—the so-called McJob. Still, in most cases it is hard to avoid the expectation that employees are entitled to benefits, particularly when the competition is offering them.

■ The Problems

The different values served by benefits lead to different ideas of what benefits are. In the context of the total compensation equation, I consider that benefits (indirect pay) are compensation, but of a form similar to insurance. Hence those programs that I suggest we include under the heading of *benefits* are those that protect the employee from future expected or possible events (health and disability insurance are examples). Other programs and "bennies," such as company cars, educational support, and child care, will be located elsewhere because they meet different types of needs—training, for example, or discounts on company products. Because the compensation area has been underconceptualized, the typical compensation taxonomy—as I mentioned in Chapter One—involves pay, benefits, and a few (if any) perks. This situation meant that everything that was not pay was located under bennies or perks.

Further, as we move forward, I take the position that the cost of benefits should not be borne only by the employer but should be shared by the employee. Employers may provide, for example, a basic package, one that can be enhanced at the employee's choice—and cost.

There are a host of problems with the kinds of benefits under discussion here that frustrate employers. Among the most important are the following:

- Employer and employee confusion about benefits
- Cost issues
- Unfunded liabilities
- Lack of employer leverage
- Administrative complexities
- Lack of customized fit and flexibility
- The issue of who gets coverage
- Gaming the system

1. Employer and Employee Confusion About Benefits

Employers and employees alike are often not sure why benefits are paid, or, from the employee's viewpoint, what benefits a worker is entitled to receive. Such confusion is typical when competing values are in play. Are benefits compensation, social insurance, or a response to what employees want? Employers don't always know, and the result is that they do not have a consistent philosophy about what benefits should be offered, how much should be allocated to benefits, and how the benefits program should be rolled out to employees. Within most firms of any size, there are employee groups and human resources personnel who differ markedly along the fault lines I have just identified.

This confusion also means that it is difficult for employers to articulate what part of the costs of which benefits they should cover, and why. Mostly, employers have played a reactive rather than proactive role in benefits. Too, many programs that help or reward employees but should be located elsewhere end up being called benefits. Paying for MBA training, for example, is often called a benefit, but is more appropriately considered as part of a package labeled "opportunity for growth."

This lack of clarity and crispness on the part of employers is matched by a similar lack of clarity in the minds of employees. But there is more confusion for employees than just the philosophical underpinnings of the program. Benefits packages are usually complex, and most of them do not come into play until something happens—illness, disability, being laid off, and so on. Because benefits are "then and there" elements rather than "here and now," most employees do not really know what benefits they have, and exactly when these benefits come into play and what they cover. In this sense most benefits are like the provisions of homeowners' insurance. Most employees know only that they have certain kinds of coverage, without knowing in detail what it includes.

2. Cost Issues

What employers *do* know is that benefits cost a bundle. Benefits now account for between 30 percent and 40 percent of salaries and wages. So, for every $1,000 in pay, employers need to allocate an additional $300 to $400 for benefits.[4] Little wonder, then, that many organizations seek to avoid paying benefits altogether, with the McJob becoming increasingly common in some of the new, nonunionized occupations. In the relentless competitive pressure to cut costs, benefits have been a natural target.

Total cost is one problem. A second problem is uncontrolled cost. Such lack of control occurs in several ways. For one thing, when an employer agrees to provide a benefit, it may initially provide more value for cost, compared to what the employees can do on their own. However, the employer is then on the hook for that benefit no matter what happens to the cost of providing it. Medical insurance is a prime example. As medical costs started rising rapidly, employers found they were facing very steep annual percentage increases just to maintain existing coverage. Employees, of course, don't appreciate the cost issue—

from their perspective, they are getting the same benefit. The fact
that it costs their employer more is irrelevant to them.

3. Unfunded Liabilities

A similar problem occurs in the retirement area. Many organizations have a *defined benefit* plan, in which a retiree is guaranteed a certain level of compensation (with appropriate
adjustments for life expectancy) for life. Firms get a sense of
what they are liable for by multiplying the compensation of current retirees by their life expectancy. As people are living longer,
firms have a huge liability developing. Some firms put resources
aside for this purpose, but it is hard to do, and companies may
skip or skimp. Too often employees have been left in the lurch
as firms failed to meet their obligations—often by going out of
business entirely.

4. Lack of Employer Leverage

To make matters even more problematic, employers feel, rightly,
that as things stand now they do not get much benefit from benefits. They are costly and they do not provide much additional
employee motivation, especially considering that they are such
a large percentage of salaries and wages. So there is little on the
plus side. On the minus side, there are administrative hassles
and costs. Further, employers face an implacable set of employee
entitlement expectations, so that employees are continually operating on the "dissatisfied" side of the ledger. ("Why can't we
have better medical, better vision, better dental, more prescrip-
tion coverage . . . ?") Zingheim and Schuster feel that benefits
lack zip. "To us, benefits just aren't an accelerator pedal to improve the chances of your company meeting its business goals
or communicating effectively about the win-win that's required
for the better workforce deal."[5]

5. Administrative Complexities

The fact that the benefits system is a kind of stepchild to the firm, poorly understood by employers and employees alike, means that it is frequently undermanaged and overadministered. The poor understanding of the larger, more strategic parts of the system means that there is lots of microwork around specific issues, employee by employee. Since the traditional system is reactive and problem-oriented, employees have no incentive to learn anything about it. Hence the "new employee orientation" in which benefits are explained is viewed with raging boredom by most employees. Then some issue comes up, and there is a spike in interest, followed by a return to boredom.

6. Lack of Customized Fit and Flexibility

The traditional benefits system arose in a more traditional time and so represented a one-size-fits-all approach. Father was at work; mother was home with 2.5 kids and a dog. Everyone was thirty-five. Of course, the picture was never that tidy, but the traditional mind-set dominated.

Today's workforce, as everyone acknowledges, is far more diverse. There are two-parent working families, single-parent families, queer families, older workers, younger workers, "differently abled" workers, and so on. Since employees' need for benefits depends much more on their cultural background and stage of life than in former decades, the traditional, fixed package does not fit everyone, by a long shot.

In fact, there is substantial question whether it fits anyone. The problem is that in providing one set of benefits, the traditional program gives medical care to those already covered, does not give enough medical care to those who need more, forces employees to save for retirement in firm-approved (and sometimes controlled) ways, and so on. Apart from the obvious problems of rigidity, the system has an un-American flavor:

in everything from dog food to 401k plans, Americans prize choice.

The traditional benefits structure lacks flexibility in another way as well. It essentially mandates that what is offered to one must be offered to all. Hence, employers have an incentive to minimize benefits packages. If some employees want pet health insurance, then everyone has to have it. As that becomes cost prohibitive, employers resist, and employees with pets join the ranks of the disaffected.

7. The Issue of Who Gets Coverage

This problem is perhaps the hardest nut of all to crack. "Of course, my family needs to be covered"—so say employees. But why *is* that? The main answers are history (we have done it in the past) and competition (others are doing it). Firms may seek to develop a more robust, well-reasoned, and effectively communicated rationale for the coverage the firm offers. The problem is that such principles are often contested. As lifestyles and expectations change, there is great debate about the extent of coverage and the costs associated with broader enrollments. For example, a plan might cover the employee and the employee's family. But even "family" is confusing, as reflected in the recent controversies that have erupted in many organizations about whether gay and lesbian partners are entitled to medical coverage. This question soon leads to others: What about an employee's live-in girlfriend or boyfriend? Are they "partners"? Or what about older children who are stuck in jobs without benefits? There is every reason to think these difficulties are only going to increase.

8. Gaming the System

Finally, there is the problem of *gaming the system,* or manipulating it to one's advantage. This is something that both organizations and employees seek to do. Some organizations will pay employees not to take their health coverage if they can go on a spouse's coverage. Meanwhile, employees with dual coverage seek to collect twice. Employers challenge every workers' compensation claim to reduce their tax; employees stretch workers' comp injuries and disabilities as ways to get "free money." The beat goes on. The policy/practice gap leads to frustration for both employers and employees.

■ Suggested Solutions

To consider some solutions to the befuddlement caused by benefits, let's first look briefly at suggestions for each of the eight problems I've listed. We'll then move to a more global solution, cafeteria benefits. We'll conclude with some considerations about assessing and improving your benefits plan.

1. Employer and Employee Confusion About Benefits

Recall that part of the issue here is the multiplicity of values or philosophies in play. Employers need to explore what mix of compensation, social insurance, and expected offerings will drive their benefits package. Most employers will come out with some combination of all three, but achieving clarity about why they are paying different sorts of benefits will help them communicate their program more effectively.

At one extreme, some employers may elect to pay all compensation in cash and let employees purchase whatever protections they wish. That is one option. Other firms feel that social insurance perspectives are vital and make providing this type of benefit part of their mission. (Ben & Jerry's was like that, with stringent ratios between top and bottom earners.) And some businesses just want to match the market and move on. The point is to explore exactly where you want your firm to be, and why. How do firms choose among, or weight, these values?

Among the factors that come to mind are the company's size, the competitive environment (geographically and by industry segment), the expectations of the available workforce, and the company's own values.

Once a policy has been clarified, a communication plan needs to be developed. The initial employee interview, thought by many firms to be the vehicle to explain benefits, usually fails on two counts. One is that new employees are so overloaded that they fail to understand even the basic plans that are presented to them. The second is that the so-called explanation usually does not deal with that most essential of all explanations—the reason why. Most of these exchanges simply provide descriptions and outlines of the plans (and often not even that), with little or no attention to the purpose of the plans and the rationale behind them. To alleviate employee confusion about benefits, employers need to have a communication plan that deals with both the how and the why. Usually, in matters of compensation, employers need to overcommunicate. Since no one kind of communication always works well with all, a mix of personal, print, and electronic communication is good, plus access through phone and intranet. Periodic reminders also help.

More than that, though, firms need to review and evaluate their communication plan for benefits and its effectiveness. For example, occasional focus groups with employees will provide a lot of information on the extent to which the message or messages are getting through. Reviewing the best communication of organizations in similar fields will also help.

2. and 3. Cost Issues and Unfunded Liabilities

At some time other than "budget time," firms should perform a full analysis of what benefits really cost.[6] Budget time, of course, is the annual work of preparing company and department budget lines. Benefits come in as one of those lines. This is a bad time to evaluate anything because everything needs to come together.

There simply is not time to look into the real costs of any item. "Real" means more than the percentage of salaries and wages; it means the full cost, including the exposures of commitments (uncontrolled costs and unfunded liabilities) as well as the administrative costs of the benefit department, unemployment compensation taxes, workers' compensation insurance premiums, and so on. Once the full cost has been estimated, companies can ask about other ways to achieve more bang for the buck.

One way to improve the cost picture—a way that reaches full expression in a cafeteria benefits program—is to move from a defined benefits plan to a defined contribution plan. In this type of plan, the employer decides (in consultation with compensation firms and employees) how much it wants to contribute to the benefit package. It then designs medical and retirement packages that move toward that goal.

4. Lack of Employer Leverage

Looking at the actual cost of benefits permits employers to explore ways in which they can achieve more leverage for the money they are spending. Among other ways to achieve greater employer value for value provided, firms may target more—and more effective—communication, program redesign, collaborative activities with other organizations to reduce costs, and closer alignments with suppliers. Some firms, for example, send employees a year-end statement outlining the value of benefits in dollars and cents. Others have training sessions on medical plans, retirement options, and the like.

5. Administrative Complexities

Even without transformational change (change of the system), transactional change (change within the system) can be achieved through simplification and streamlining of the benefits program. Over time, most organizations have a substantial policy/practice gap in the area of benefits. Because of the problems I have already mentioned, exceptions are made here, exceptions are made there, and the gap widens. Organizational lore about special cases soon develops, changing benefits administration from being policy driven to being case-law driven.

I alluded in Chapter Four to Occam's Razor, the principle that among competing mathematical proofs the proof with the fewest steps wins. The application to benefits is that the simpler program is the better program. Lots of underbrush can be cleared away from most programs, even without a major overhaul of the system. For example, because of the lack of communication review, many firms have outdated and inaccurate print materials. For many employees, these materials are so far from reality that it is not possible to understand the available benefits from them. Too, fears of legal action cause firms to enmesh their print text in every kind of small print, turning off many employees. These employees are then forced to go to the benefits office to get "the latest"—only to be informed inaccurately by a new benefits officer who has yet to be trained. And so it goes. Firms can, should, and must do better.

6. Lack of Customized Fit and Flexibility

The problem that drives the policy/practice gap is the combination of a rigid system and a diverse workforce. Firms do seek to accommodate their employees' diverse needs, but a rigid system permits only exceptions, backdoor arrangements, and one-of-a-kind decisions. The result is that a bramble bush of actual practices develops. Programs that build in choice—and cafeteria benefits is the program that does this best—can allow the employee to customize a personal package.

7. The Issue of Who Gets Coverage

Because of the contested social values in this area, most firms are probably best off following the market. There will always be market leaders—firms that add new benefits (gay and lesbian partner health coverage, for example) that, in time, become accepted practice. On average, though, offering a conventional package may be the best way to sidestep controversy and most criticism. There will always be benefits that people want, but not all benefits can be offered. Another solution, and one that addresses a number of employer and employee concerns, is to move to a cafeteria benefits plan.

8. Gaming the System

Gaming the system can be converted, as it were, to a source of system improvement. If employers track the kinds of exceptions that employees seek and eliminate the illegal ones, that information can be one of the most valuable sources of policy changes. For example, at many companies, sick time is an issue. Employers have found, though, that many employees take sick time when children, rather than they themselves, are sick. It turns out that combining vacation time, sick time, and so on into a total package gives both employees and employer a better handle on what the array of time is—and it also helps employees feel better about using the available time and therefore more satisfied with their jobs.

■ A Transformational Solution: Cafeteria Benefits

One of the better transformational changes that firms can make is to adopt a cafeteria benefits plan.[7] Such plans—sometimes called *flex benefits*—have been around since the 1970s, but are becoming increasingly popular, ranging from full flex (everything can be chosen) through medium flex (some things can be chosen, others are prescribed) to miniflex (just a few things can be chosen). In all cases the principle—the same principle that is the basis of cafeteria compensation—is customization and choice.

Employees have the ability to configure, within a dollar limit, the kind of benefits package they wish to have for a given year. As their life changes, so their benefits can change. If employees want a higher-end benefit, many plans offer it for purchase with salary dollars. For example, if a firm offers an auto insurance feature (probably cheaper than an employee can buy as an individual, as a result of the bulk negotiations), the flex plan could allow employees to draw on salary dollars to pay for it. It could also allow employees who don't need medical coverage because they are covered by a spouse's plan to redirect the dollars not used for this purpose to buy the auto insurance.

Employees like cafeteria plans because they allow this kind of choice and flexibility. Employers like cafeteria plans because they limit the employer's contributions. It sounds like a win-win. And it is, in a way. But there are issues—value conflicts—and problems.

On the issue side, a cafeteria plan changes the nature of benefits in a fundamental way. It moves from a social insurance model to a compensation model and from a defined benefit approach to a defined contribution approach. What this change means is that employers now have a specific "cost" for benefits (defined contribution), rather than being on the hook for whatever the benefits cost (defined benefit). I believe that these changes have positive consequences for employer and employee alike. They help the employer manage costs, they make employees more aware of exactly what they are getting, and they force each employee to take some responsibility for picking what benefits go into the package. In addition, because these plans limit employer cost, they can free up some money for accomplishment-based pay. These are good things, in my view—but not everyone agrees. Others feel that a cafeteria plan reneges on commitments made by employers and puts the employee at inappropriate risk. These differences are real, but the trend is toward cafeteria plans.

There are also some problems—or implementation consideration, at any rate. For one thing, the transition from the old to the new approach can be complex, and usually requires the assistance of a consulting firm with relevant experience. Lots of employee involvement is one of the key requisites of a successful transition. Larger firms find it easier to provide a cafeteria plan than smaller ones do, because the larger firms have greater human resources capacity already within the organization. Additionally, firms need to decide what kind of plan they want— full flex, partial flex—and deal with some specific administrative problems. One of the most often mentioned is the problem of *adverse selection*. This concern arises from the possibility that, if changes are permitted each year, employees will only select those things that they need in that year. So, for example, people who wear glasses will select the vision part of the program only in the year when they need glasses. (One of the virtues of the social insurance model was that it did spread the risk!) This particular problem can be addressed by identifying those areas most subject to adverse selection (vision and orthodontia are two examples) and setting up controls so that employees cannot enter and exit those specific areas every year. A two- to three-year enrollment seems to work well until firm-specific experience is developed.

There are problems, of course, with any plan. But one that clarifies employer and employee responsibilities is a fine way to go. As you may know, cafeteria plans do not wind up costing less, at least initially, because employers are loath to appear to reduce benefits that are currently offered. The problems that the cafeteria approach solves, though—taking the employer off the hook for the benefit and substituting a cash equivalent—sets up a more promising future in several ways. One is that it allows the employer to "cost share" future increases with employees. While this has some negative aspects from an employee's perspective, I believe that the involvement it creates on the part of employees is very beneficial. It is appropriate for employees to become involved in their own compensation—and benefits are a part of it.

Finally, as cafeteria benefits plans are implemented and operated, they are a good way to begin the process of moving toward a total (cafeteria) compensation plan. This is another plus for the cafeteria benefits approach.[8]

■ Assessing Your Benefits Plan

Part of the message of this book is that all the elements of compensation need to be part of a single integrated and flexible system. Because cafeteria compensation is a larger version of cafeteria benefits, a good place to start on the road to a total compensation and rewards system is in the benefits area. Here are a few hints on how to proceed.

1. *Start where the senior staff is.* My experience suggests that too often only the person directly in charge of benefits really knows in detail what is in the package. So a first step in thinking about benefits is to ask senior staff several questions:

- What are the benefits we offer now?
- What do they really cost us?
- Do we feel we get a benefit from benefits? Is the benefit proportionate to the cost?
- Are there benefits we do not need anymore?
- Are there benefits we would like to offer that are not currently in the package?

2. *Ask the director of benefits.* To get a sense of how accurate (or, more likely, inaccurate) the senior people are, ask the person in charge of benefits to review your answers. Locate and record the areas of greatest confusion or inaccuracy.

3. *Explore other issues with the director of benefits.* The person in charge of the benefits program probably knows about problem areas that you haven't thought of. Ask what they are. Find out whether you match, lead, or lag the competition.

4. *Get employee input.* Through surveys and focus groups, ask employees what they like and dislike about the current benefits program. Asking whether they would like more choice in their benefits package could help pave the way for a cafeteria plan.

5. *Explore some best practices.* Inquire what other firms are doing. The answers may not be what you would expect. For example, consider the health plan at Merrill Lynch:

> There are heath plans and there are health plans. And then there is Merrill Lynch & Co.'s health plan. By just about any standard the financial giant is generous in what it covers. . . . The company regularly retools its coverage to accommodate special needs. . . . But here's the really odd part: The company says its approach appears to be saving money. Adjusted for inflation, its health costs have declined even while others have expanded. And Merrill spends less per employee than many similarly sized companies. In fact, a half-dozen other corporations have copied its health plan.[9]

How does Merrill Lynch achieve such results? Part of the answer seems to be that the company is saving money by focusing on early detection and clinical excellence. In addition—and here is an example of gainsharing in the benefits program—instead of coveting all the gains, the company uses some of them to provide enriched benefits. It's an approach that is worth thinking about.

6. *Revisit your policy.* With solid data in hand, hold a policy council meeting involving whatever players are needed to make a change in the benefits package. Strive to gain clarity on the values you want the benefits program to serve and the payoff you expect from it. Listen to the employee input. Don't be afraid to

rethink the concept of what benefits should be offered. Remember Merrill Lynch. Adding some higher-end options may seem counterintuitive but have payoff.

7. *Communicate, communicate, communicate.* Remember that any change involving pay—or part of pay—is a cultural one. Everyone, from front-line employees to senior staff, needs to understand the ideas and purposes behind this—and any—change. Overcommunication (saying it again and again) and layered communication (saying it in different media) are very helpful.

8. *Do it all again.* One of the lessons of this chapter is that this kind of review needs to happen regularly. Benefits should be reviewed and improved yearly. Part of the reason for this is that in a Web-year society the old "two years to improve the employee handbook" approach is simply unacceptable. (The employee handbooks are now electronic—frequently Web-based.) Part of the reason why updating has been so slow is that the one-size-fits-all approach has created a fixed superstructure that makes change monumental. Hence we avoid the task; hence, when we have to do it, it becomes a major pain in the ass.

Metaphorically, most compensation systems are like most business buildings—large, fixed structures. Changing (moving things around, for instance) becomes limited by the architecture. Suppose one started with the idea of flexibility, and built x thousand square feet with movable walls—Alcoa's new headquarters in Pittsburgh is like this; change would then be much easier. I am suggesting, then, yearly adjustments. Part of this change is keeping up with the market proactively, as opposed to letting the market bang you on the head. Then you can use intramural and extramural sources of information to help. Employee surveys—e-mail can help here, as can the Web—can give you good information. Plus the requests for exceptions that employees make can help suggest new needs that might be addressed. That is on the intramural side. Looking outward, best practices and information from places like WorldatWork can give a state of the field perspective. Someone from HR is dedicated to this task so it is not left hanging. And fine-tuning can occur on an ongoing basis. In fact, in flexibility-based systems the "full scale review" becomes fine-tuning.

CHAPTER SUMMARY

Benefits, or what I have termed indirect pay, became a major part of the compensation scene during World War II as a way to provide a kind of income to employees during a period of wage controls. They have since grown to a substantial chunk of total compensation costs. This growth occurred for both business reasons and social reasons.

As the workforce and the competitive environment changes, benefits programs need to be reviewed regularly and thoroughly. A combination of a traditional, rigid system and a diverse workforce is a recipe for both discontent and major policy/practice gaps.

Employers need to be as clear about the values they want their benefits program to serve as they are (or should be) about what the program costs. It also falls to employers to communicate the rationale as well as the specifics of the benefits program to employees.

Cafeteria benefits plans address a number of the concerns reviewed in this chapter by increasing the scope of employee choice, limiting the employer's contribution, and increasing the flexibility in the system. It is, in fact, a logical step from this concept to the idea of cafeteria compensation promoted in this book. Despite the logic, this development has been a long time in coming. As far back as 1983, research showed that the cafeteria concept was a good one because of the wide variation in employee preferences.[10]

Works-Pay and Perks-Pay

Acquiring Tools, Achieving Status

T he next two elements in the total compensation equation are works-pay and perks-pay. *Works-pay* is my term for anything that the employer provides employees for their work that they would otherwise have to purchase themselves— uniforms, equipment, desks, computers, cell phones, cars—as well as any tools necessary for doing the job. *Perks-pay* refers to perquisites, ranging from discounts on company products to club memberships. Works-pay and perks-pay provide, respectively, tools and status.

With works-pay and perks-pay we move into a hazy area of compensation. These forms of compensation are not exactly money, but they are not exactly non-money either. Works-pay and perks-pay are like international currency exchanges: corporate cash is used to support workers in their work, to entice them to use company products (or to feel good about where they work), or to enhance their prestige and self-esteem.

What do works-pay and perks-pay have to do with the total compensation equation? Quite a bit, actually, but they work in different directions. Without works-pay, employees would have to buy necessary materials, in effect reducing their income. Firms may have a resource-rich or resource-poor environment with respect to employees. Some provide everything people need to do the job—and then some; others are cheap and make employees buy or grovel for every jot and tittle. The same salary is worth less at the second type of firm than at the first. I once consulted for a firm that would not give employees a yellow pad unless they turned in the cardboard from the old one!

Perks, on the other hand, enhance or boost pay, or make it worth more in lifestyle terms. Perks are preferred access to goods and services at the cost of the company. As I will mention, the most common perk is a discount on company products, where the product can work in this way (auto companies can give a discount on their products; steel companies cannot). For employees who like the company's product, this can be valuable. Other perks provide signature rewards—trips, parking places, and so on—that signal to employees that the recipients are special.

■ Works-Pay: Personal and Workplace

In general, I use works-pay to refer to the tangible supplies and equipment people need to do their jobs. Elements such as association memberships that enhance people's ability to do the job in a more general way (largely through learning) I locate under "opportunity for growth." High-end equipment—a prestige car, for example—begins to move toward perks-pay. It is somewhat more than is needed to do the job.

I further characterize works-pay tools and materials as job-related rather than career-related. *Job-related* refers to the job a person is doing now; *career-related* refers to that job plus the next one. Job-related equipment is not usually portable in the way career-related elements are.[1]

Works-pay can be divided into two types: personal works-pay and workplace works-pay. The former includes the items the individual worker uses or has possession of from day to day. The latter refers to the equipment and conditions of the workplace setting. Pens, pencils, uniforms, and portable tools are personal works-pay; desks, computers, cubicles, and forklifts are workplace works-pay.

With both types of works-pay, there are, naturally, differences of opinion about what counts as *needed*. Perhaps all employers and employees can agree on the minimum materials required. I am reminded, though, of the window washer who said, "My company makes me buy all my equipment except ladders." Clearly, other things are required for the job, such as cleaning supplies. The firm's argument was that the window washers were sloppy with cleaning supplies if they belonged to the company and that their behavior would be more economical if they had to purchase the disposable supplies. Since, as with base pay, employers tend to regard works-pay as a cost to be minimized, they frequently try to spend as little as possible and offload some costs onto the workers. Employers who do this fail to realize that a well-equipped worker has an extra measure of readiness, both technologically and attitudinally, to do the job. On the other hand, workers may tend to overstate what they need to accomplish their tasks.

There are other problems with works-pay besides conflicting definitions of *necessary*. Let's consider problems and suggested solutions for each type of works-pay.

Personal Works-Pay

Personal works-pay—the tools that individual workers need to do their work, and to improve in their work—includes items such as the following:

- *Personal outfitting:* clothes, uniforms, protective gear, and so on
- *Tools:* everything from hammers to cell phones to software, as well as backup systems such as a home computer or an e-mail and Internet access account
- *Supplies:* Post-it notes, pens, and other routine supply closet items
- *Entertainment:* reimbursements for business lunches, power breakfasts, and the like

Employers may provide for these needs in a number of ways, such as through a company store, a reimbursement process, or a corporate credit card. Employees are not infrequently stuck with at least part of the bill: the MBA students I teach spend between $100 and $2,000 per year on materials and resources like the ones just listed.

Problems with Personal Works-Pay

There are several issues involved in personal works-pay. First, there are differences of opinion about essential versus enhanced tools and equipment. Take, for example, a home computer system. A number of workers today argue that they need redundant systems to respond more quickly to customers and suppliers alike, particularly as business goes national and global. The San Francisco employee, for example, is just getting up at 6 A.M., a time when New York compeers have been at work for an hour already. One could require the employee to come into the office on Eastern Standard Time so as to facilitate communication, but a home computer would allow much smoother access.

A second issue returns us to investment versus cost. Materials necessary to the job certainly are a cost, but they are also an investment. That is why it might be a good idea to tie an employee's ability to purchase tools (for example, through a company account) to some measure of personal productivity. Under such a system, however, the more productive employee would get more supplies, a bigger computer screen, and so on. We might think of the differences here as "basis" works-pay (what everyone gets) and "enhanced" or "preferred" works-pay. On one hand, it makes sense to provide more to those who produce more. On the other, the allocation of basis and enhanced works raises issues of fairness and the degree of individuation that such a program may develop.

A third issue concerns taste and preference. Some people like the toys. Take telephones for one example. A firm may provide a basic model of desk phone for every employee; perhaps support staff have more lines, but the basic phone is what everyone gets. For many this provision might be fine. For others, though, a hands-free or portable model, one with bells and whistles, might be just the thing they want. Should the employer provide it? How is the determination of necessity developed? When should an employee's wishes be taken into account?

Finally, it's worth noting the issue of whether an employee can keep personal works-pay tools. When my redundant home computer is replaced, and has been expensed by my employer, can I keep it for myself or my mom?

Suggested Solutions for Personal Works-Pay

The first element firms need to consider in connection with personal works-pay is the inventory question: what, exactly, do we now provide, to whom, and on what basis? My experience suggests that the answer to this question will be all over the lot. Some things are provided across the board, others not, still others if an employee asks, and so on. Different departments and different areas of the business may have different practices even if there is a policy—and frequently there is not. An inventory is a key first step. It will tell you what is available, and under what conditions.

Step two involves organizing the practices into a coherent form: here are the tools we currently provide, to whom, and on what basis. Then a management team can review these practices and see whether they seem reasonable, consistent, fair, business-related, profit producing, and so on. Nothing should be done with this review, however, until step three.

Step three involves asking employees whether they think the patterns the employer has uncovered actually represent what happens. In most cases there will be some adjustment as employees say, for example, "Well, yes, that does happen—occasionally—but it takes us so long to get the work aprons that most of us buy them ourselves." Then employees can be asked what necessities are not being provided. In a fast-changing Web-year environment (a Web-year is three months), what is needed in the way of processes and tools is a moving target. Consider software upgrades as one case in point. But there are other elements that matter—office organization, for example. What "goes with" the employee in the sense of a package that is provided initially and upgraded regularly? One of the executives I interviewed gave the following example, which makes the point crisply: "Around here you might or might not get additional equipment. I wanted a home fax—I get material from our East Coast office—and I need to send them things—and working from home is a necessity. It was a successful request—no problem, in fact. But Jim in commercial loans was not successful. His manager just 'couldn't see it.' Whatever that means. So it's a horse race."

Step four involves comparing the management review with the employee input and developing a series of policies and practices that will help employees get the tools they really need, quickly and without hassles. At the same time, these policies should establish a mechanism for acquiring the necessities. An employee works-pay account is one such mechanism. With a standard amount for a defined job and possible bumps for outstanding performance, both universal and unique issues can be addressed. Employers can score some extra points by offering such an account up front, as a thoughtful addition to the recruitment and retention package, rather than being forced into it.

Workplace Works-Pay

Whereas personal works-pay refers to tools that the individual personally uses, workplace works-pay refers to those tangible necessities that are part of the workplace itself. Typically, unlike personal works-pay, individual workers cannot buy or provide workplace equipment themselves.

In discussing workplace works-pay, it is convenient to divide the workplace into three levels: micro, meso, and macro. It is the micro level that falls most directly into the compensation area. Micro-level works-pay refers to the cubicle, stand, or specific area of the plant where an employee does the daily tasks. Here again, the point is to have resources available that are necessary for employees to do the job and that they would otherwise have to pay for, thus reducing their pay.

The question here is how the employer equips the work space. I recall one professor friend saying, "I have the same metal desk I had when I began in the 1960s." He works at a college where there is no policy for outfitting and upgrading his work space. When he came they gave him a desk, and he has had that desk ever since. Never mind that office furniture has improved dramatically in the last thirty years. I suppose he could buy a new desk for himself, but that might seem a bit much. Employees expect employers to provide them with current, safe, and comfortable equipment in their workplace environment, and to foot the bill.

Bosses often miss what is important. I once consulted with an entrepreneur who was angry because some of the support staff were complaining about their chairs. "They want expensive chairs that pump up and down and back and forth," he fumed. "They cost five hundred dollars. Regular chairs are good enough for me, and should be good enough for them." It fell to me to point out that, in fact, he did not have a "regular chair"; he had an executive chair that cost several times what the employees were asking for. At that, he was up and down all day and did not do any typing. I shared with him that, as someone who typed a good deal, I readily understood the employees' ergonomic concerns. I urged him to take the high road and allow staffers the chance to choose their own chairs so that they could customize a key piece of their work environment. After some more fuming, he followed my suggestion. The staff had fun getting the chairs, productivity zoomed, and absences fell.

The meso and the macro area are not, strictly speaking, compensation as I have defined it—things that the employee would otherwise have to buy to do the job. I want to discuss them here, however, because they fall into the continuum of things that the employer can do to attract and retain employees. If employees have to cut their own pay to work at a firm, they are less likely to do it, or they will work less—or steal from the employer—to make themselves whole. If the employees have to work with poor equipment in their area or plant, they are more likely to look for work elsewhere or to demand higher wages.

The meso level is the work region, such as one's floor or office area. Here is where larger equipment comes into play: the photocopy machine, the filing room, the drill press. The meso area is also where meeting rooms are located and teleconference facilities, speakerphones, and the like are available. At the meso level it is really not possible for employees to buy their own upgrades.

The macro area is the whole plant or firm. Is the equipment up to date and functional? Is it ergonomically sound? Is the lighting adequate without being harsh? Is the air healthy? Are there enough people to do the job without undue strain? Consider an airline example. Flying out of Detroit as I do, I have the opportunity to talk with a number of airline employees about their work and how they feel about it. One airline in particular always seems to have long lines of customers waiting to be served. The counter is perennially understaffed, as is the luggage office downstairs. The employees tell me that they do not feel good about working for this company because it is chronically understaffed. They feel they cannot offer the service they have been trained to provide; the bench strength is just not there.

Problems with Workplace Works-Pay

An overall problem with workplace works-pay lies in the area of employer review and decision making about what, exactly, will be provided, and how it will be maintained and upgraded. Employers frequently do not perform such reviews, operating reactively in a crisis-driven mind-set. Further, employers need to be sure which parts of the equipment are most central to the productive workplace. We all have seen employers who upgrade a "whatsis" that has no relevance to employees, while machinery that could really help them do their jobs is held together with baling wire. One wonders about the lack of insight that leads employers to overlook the possibility of asking the employees what they need. One of my editors shared a couple of anecdotes that illustrate this point.

> Some years ago a publishing company I worked for was expanding its office space by taking over a second floor in the building. Management decided to make this new space a showcase, presumably one that the production editors, designers, and other worker bees would love. Alas, executives sometimes know as much about workers, even in a small company like this one, as Marie Antoinette knew about peasants. The

chosen method for designing the space was to call on an interior decorator—not an interior designer, mind, but a decorator. Thousands of dollars were invested in "executive-style" desks, soft lighting, plush chairs, color coordination, and so on.

After the employees moved into their new diggings, it took about an hour to discover that the space was completely dysfunctional. No one had thought to put in electric outlets for essential equipment. Workers who routinely had to swivel around from desk to computer to telephone found that their chairs were all but immobile. The handsome desks were the wrong size for dealing with galley proofs and other tools of the trade. The lighting was wrong for close work on proofs. And, of all things, bookcases were lacking.

The company got it right the second time: the space was remodeled again, but this time they put one of their own employees in charge, a woman who happened to be skilled in interior design as well as book design (and who, of course, had been there all along, but had never been consulted). Not only did she call on her own knowledge of what the work required, but she was careful to interview other employees.

An executive at another publishing house, which happened to be an arm of "Regular Oil," routinely brought down the house at publishing meetings by recounting how workspace amenities were determined at his place of employment. It seems that Regular Oil had a, well, regular way of allocating space and equipment based on rank in the company. If you were a second vice president, you got an office of a certain size, a certain type of desk, even a specified size of ash tray. The system might have worked tolerably well for the oil executives, but for someone charged with publishing responsibilities—to say nothing of a nonsmoker—none of it worked. Among other things, this particular second vice president needed tabletop space on which to spread layouts, proofs, and the like. But tailoring the workspace to actual needs was something that simply wasn't done.

Some macro-level elements are in dispute. Parking is one example. While the bosses at the University of Michigan consider it a cost of business to give me an office and a desk, files, a computer, and so on (though they did not give me a typewriter when that was standard), they charge for parking. Apparently, like other employers, they feel that getting to work is my problem, while working at work is more in their domain. Other firms, of course, provide free parking for their employees. So one question is, where does the workplace end?

This problem surfaces for the rapidly growing work-at-home group as well. What responsibilities, if any, should the employer assume if the employee telecommutes? Such an employee may require a fax machine, for example, whereas those in the office can use the communal fax. (This issue came up in cross-country offices, mentioned a bit ago.) This and other costs add up.

Some materials can be both personal works-pay and workplace works-pay. Ford's decision to give each employee a computer and Internet access was based in part on the idea that computer skills are increasingly essential in today's workplace. Further, Ford figured—shrewdly, I think—that employees would self-train (or, more likely, be trained by their kids), thus saving the company some training and retraining costs.

Another problem worth considering is the transition point when works-pay becomes perks-pay. Perks, as we shall see in a moment, usually have the role of creating status impressions and distinctions. A company car, for example, may be a necessity; a company luxury car may not be (although the luxury part may come under "perks-pay").

Suggested Solutions for Workplace Works-Pay
I need not dwell on suggestions for workplace works-pay in detail, since the same series of steps that were useful in personal works-pay are useful here as well. There are a couple of other issues to consider, however. One of them is scope. Workplace

works-pay involves substantial dollars. We are talking about buildings, big construction, lots of cubicles, lots of computers. That means big cost, a subject that always makes employers nervous. While there is nothing wrong with trying to reduce major costs, we have all seen lots of penny-wise but pound-foolish decisions made. Hence, I would urge employers to regard works-pay investments (note the choice of word) in state-of-the-art equipment, workplace design, and technology as a chance to obtain competitive advantage. Employees want to be on the leading edge. If an employer is running an antiquated shop, it is no wonder when people start leaving. Moreover, the cost of being out of date is being hidden in the employee replacement budget and in lost productivity. So the message is, Upgrade as frequently as you can afford, and watch out for costs in the status quo that may outweigh the sticker price on new equipment.

On a personal works-pay level, one way the employer might approach the problem is to authorize each employee to spend up to a certain amount on such items. The employees can then choose what they wish to get over and above the basis package the employer provides for specific jobs and job families.

■ Perks-Pay

Perks are special privileges that one is entitled to as a result of working for a particular organization or having a particular position within that organization. What Richard Henderson has said about "employee services" provides a beginning definition of perks: "compensation components that enable the employee to enjoy a better lifestyle or meet social and personal obligations while minimizing employer-related costs."[2] He goes on to talk about "income equivalent payments" and points out that employees often find them highly desirable and both employers and employees find them tax-beneficial, although the IRS is requiring that "a specific portion of certain perks be considered income to employees."[3] The *general perk* is of this sort. Typically it involves giving discounts on company products. The University of Michigan, for example, lets faculty and students buy football tickets at a reduced price. Automobile companies typically have car purchase discount plans for their employees. Retail outlets usually provide a discount to their employees. And so on. This type of perk is simply the provision of goods and services at reduced cost. It is a perk because it does not apply to people outside the firm. Other general perks include such things as physical exams, access to company seminars, and so on. Here is a sample from *Wired News* of some perks in Silicon Valley companies:[4]

Sun Microsystems
- Dry cleaning
- The Sun Store, a drugstore-like affair with photo processing and floral arrangements
- Cafeteria and bistro with table service
- On-site oil change and corporate auto detailing
- Electric-car recharging dock (at the Menlo Park office)
- Injury clinics with physical therapists
- Company gym
- Lactation rooms for nursing mothers

Oracle
- Dry cleaning
- Company gym offering nail service and massages
- Parking garage and car detailing
- Florist that delivers
- Photo services
- ATMs
- Shoe repair
- Six different restaurants with cuisines ranging from American to Indian

Netscape
- Dry cleaning
- Company gym
- Car detailing
- Office concierges who arrange errands and travel plans
- On-site dental care
- Photo services
- Chair massage

Intuit
- Dry cleaning
- Chair massage
- Oil change
- On-site notary services
- Laundry services
- Weekly visit from an organic fruit and veggie truck

Adaptec
- On-site massage
- Dry cleaning
- Florist
- Car detailing and oil change
- Tickets to movies and events
- Concierge to arrange travel plans and errands

A couple of the companies on this list offer a perk that has recently become popular, a concierge service. The concierge (who usually has several assistants) will (often for a small fee) make bookings to plays, find hard-to-get seats, pick up laundry, and so forth. Originally, the thinking was that many executives were asking their secretaries to attend to these tasks. Apart from the impropriety of this sort of request, many support staffers do not know how to do some of the tasks they are asked to accomplish, such as getting the hard-to-find seats. If they could do it at all, it took too much time away from their regular jobs. Hence the concierge, which has become a general perk. Merrill Lynch is joining the perks parade, and adding a new fitness center as well. (The firm is also allowing investment bankers to invest in New Economy companies while they are still private, giving them privileged access to growth opportunities).[5]

The key element involved in the general perk is that it has an across-the-board application and so does not have the effect of creating status differences among employees or enhancing the egos of the recipients. These two consequences are characteristic of the remaining perks, and one of the reasons why, except for top executives, they are in decline. I call these *special perks*. They can be divided into three groups: internal, external, and personal.

Internal perks are things to which an employee has access while inside the company facility (or just outside, as in preferred parking). Their purpose is to create distance or difference between those employees who have access to a given perk and those who do not. Special dining rooms, elevators, and bathrooms fall into this category. So does accessorizing particular employees with carpets, special office treatments, exotic decorations, or extra personal assistants and staff (such as a personal chef).

External perks are privileges used for conducting company business off site. Such perks are meant to convey enhanced personal value to the recipient and—both directly, and indirectly through the recipient—to the customer or supplier. First-class plane travel, spouse travel, chauffeur service, a prestige company car, substantial entertainment allowances, and club memberships are all examples of external perks.

Personal perks are privileges that are life- or status-enhancing and that are not connected directly to doing business. Examples include low-cost personal loans, free tax and legal advice, personal and legal counseling, free home repairs, and personal use of company facilities and equipment (for weddings and so on). Some of these may, in some companies, be general perks.

Perks are not, at the moment, considered part of earned income, but in many cases the company has to value certain perks for the IRS and report them. The recipient pays taxes on that value.

Problems

General perks really have no problems associated with them as such. Usually they represent a relatively inexpensive way for employers to give employees a break. In the case of company discounts, general perks also help to get the company's products into the market. Employees, if they value the place they work and the products it makes, often want to use the products they had a hand in making. To do so at a discount seems like a win-win. However, there is cross-company pressure on this kind of perk. Not all firms doing the same kind of thing provide the same perks. In addition, some firms make products—chemical weapons, for example—that they would not want to provide employees at any price. And then there is the issue of who, really, is a member of the organization. In the era of the boundaryless organization, where do the discounts stop? And, to recall an issue we considered in connection with indirect pay, if you give a discount to your employee, is it only for the employee, or is it also for a spouse or partner, for parents, kids, aunts, uncles? For these reasons some experts advise getting rid of perks. "Pay well," they say, "and let employees buy what they want."

A second problem with perks is that the very purpose of special perks—enhancing the status of some employees and not others—is out of sync with the contemporary American workplace and with workplaces worldwide. At a time when companies are talking teams, flatter organizations, and everyone working together, it makes sense to minimize status distinctions, not enhance them.

The third problem is the ego enlargement that goes with special perks and the difficulties that can occur as the recipients begin to believe that they really deserve these accoutrements, that they really *are* better than others. At a certain point—when the "perkee's" head will not fit through the doorjamb—the recipient becomes arrogant, demanding, infantile, bullish. Further, the more perks people get, the more perks they want.[6]

A fourth problem, which can be connected with the preceding one, is abuse of perks. First-class travel may be allowed, but that does not mean it is required. Expenses for entertainment are allowed, but that does not mean they need to be lavish. Frequent flyer miles are an example. Although allowing employees to keep their frequent flyer miles might be a good general perk, a fair number of employees do their business scheduling to maximize those frequent flyer miles, at the expense of efficiency, cost, and productivity.[7]

Suggested Solutions

My first suggestion is to provide general perks. General perks give everyone a sense of common specialness. They can bind the whole organization together rather than creating cleavages within the organization. So, for example, I think that all organizations should give employees a discount on any products that are legal to sell and useful to private individuals. It makes sense, it's cost-effective, and it gets the product out there. Also, companies can get useful feedback about their products from employees, perhaps more so than from others. If your product does not "perk-olate," you could offer one connected to another industry, such as a retail discount at selected stores.

I would also be in favor of casting a wide net with respect to perks. While not including everyone, some family members and some suppliers could be considered as well. The wider the net, the less the divisiveness.

Some firms, as I have mentioned, cannot (as opposed to will not) provide the general perk of discounts. Because general perks have exactly the opposite effect of special perks, I suggest that these firms create other categories of perks, such as a gym, special company trips, and the like. These will help provide a sense of wholeness for the organization and a sense of membership in an enterprise that can foster high performance.

My second suggestion is to avoid special perks—internal, external, or personal—as much as possible. They create divisiveness, bloat the egos of recipients, and, like many addictions, require an increasing dosage. I think I am arguing uphill here, as executives particularly like the validation that perks provide—and competitors may be offering them. Hence eliminating them completely is unrealistic. But I urge firms to think about the divisiveness that perks generate, and urge executives to think about the firm rather than themselves.

Especially important to avoid are internal and personal perks. These tend to build the most intense resentment. External perks, such as club memberships, are more acceptable and less divisive because they more clearly relate to doing business and are not "in your face," as internal perks are. Hence, if one needs to offer some special perks, then the external perk might be a compromise.

Overall, because of tax issues and divisiveness issues, perks are on the decline, except in the executive suite, where CEOs seem to relish them. One way to think about perks—general perks in particular—in a compensation framework is to outline them as part of the compensation package. Hence employees can always know that this is a part of their compensation. Then employers can decide whether to let employees take the cash value instead of the specific perks on offer. For example, an imputed, or average, value can be given to the perk—say a product discount worth $100—and employees can have that or the $100 it is worth. Employers would probably prefer not to give the cash—after all, if they stick with the discount, all employees can enjoy the idea that it's there but not all will take advantage of it, so the company gets the emotional mileage without bearing the whole cost. Here is an example of a differential approach. Some colleges and universities give no preferred rates to employees and their families who wish to attend. Others give preferred rates but only at their own institution. Still others provide cash—equivalent to their tuition—for employees and their families to attend elsewhere if they do not attend the host institution. None, to my knowledge, let you cash out the perk.

CHAPTER SUMMARY

Works-pay and perks-pay are important and often neglected parts of the total compensation program. They are important because of their impact. In different ways, the absence of adequate works-pay and the presence of special perks create problems. On the other hand, a well-thought-out program that attends to both personal and workplace works-pay provides an important element of compensation and communicates to employees that they are valued enough to be given the resources they need to do their best. General perks build togetherness through a shared participation in special features that firm members enjoy.

In tackling this area of compensation, the first step is once again to inventory your existing programs. What do you offer? Who decides what aspects of it? Does it provide what employees need and want? What connection does it have to the firm's goals?

As a next step, consider forming a works-pay and perks-pay committee of employees who can evaluate what is currently in place, determine best practices, and make recommendations for change.

It may seem a bit odd to think of works-pay and perks-pay as forms of compensation. However, in the works-pay area, the expenses the company either absorbs or passes along to the workers can be significant, while perks allow employees to enjoy an enhanced lifestyle at reduced cost, thus effectively increasing their pay. Given their implications for overall compensation, there is no reason why these areas should not be integrated into a total compensation solution.

Personal Advancement and Growth

The Ladder or the Lattice?

The compensation that firms provide employees goes beyond money. As we saw in Chapter Six, compensation can include expenses that the organization picks up in lieu of the employees' having to pay, as well as status rewards and both general and special benefits. In this chapter, we focus on two other variables that are extremely important to employees: opportunity for advancement and opportunity for growth. When employees consider working at a firm, the up-front considerations are usually base pay, opportunities for various kinds of augmented pay, and both works-pay and perks-pay. However, the extent to which the firm provides an opportunity to get ahead and an opportunity to learn is not far behind. Indeed, for some young employees it is the deal maker or deal breaker. And today, opportunity for personal growth and learning—portable compensation that can go with you—is becoming more important than opportunity for advancement.

■ From Ladder to Lattice

Historically, opportunity for advancement—moving up the career ladder—was king of the hill. That was true for a couple of reasons. One of them was that success tended to be defined in terms of achieving a higher-level position and, correlatively, with the speed at which that higher level was attained. Hence, getting to a higher level more quickly and at a younger age was better than achieving a higher level later and more slowly. The old goal—and how anachronistic it now sounds—was to make your age in thousands of dollars of salary; now the goal is about five times your age! But there was no question that higher was better.

In a few places, colleges, universities, and chamber music groups among them, higher not only wasn't considered better but was somehow suspect. Professors said things like, "I've been sentenced to be a dean." But folks like these were widely considered odd. For most everyone else, higher was better because hierarchy was where it was at, and higher and hierarchy have a lot more in common than just the sound.

Today, though, that picture has changed and is rapidly changing even more. For one thing, flatter organizations mean that there simply aren't the numbers of vice presidencies that there were in the past. To a certain extent, the career lattice has therefore replaced the career ladder. Horizontal moves, slightly upward moves, moves into different sectors with similar responsibilities—all previously viewed as undesirable—are becoming increasingly desirable. Along with the organizational lattice comes organizational *learning* as something valued more than the organizational ladder. Employees are increasingly looking at organizations from the perspective of their pedagogical or teaching capacity. *This* job needs to help you here and now, *and* prepare you for the *next* job.

When people stayed at one organization for pretty much their whole working life, job-related knowledge tended to be fairly specific. Although there were certainly technical aspects to it, the increasingly important knowledge for the single-employer individual had to do with unique aspects of the organizational culture, and job knowledge was only minimally transferable. In the new organization, where people are moving in and out all the time, core knowledge, at least, is very transferable, and customization can occur on the site. Hence, employees are looking for places to work that are good teachers. They're looking for assignment mixes that broaden and deepen their own portable skill set.

Employers, the dumb ones anyway, take a dim view of this approach. They argue, "Why should we train Harriet when she'll just leave us?" Admittedly, there is a certain risk there. Yet a trained Harriet is better for the firm now, whatever she does or does not do later.

Employers frequently talk "trust" and "commitment" when it comes to employees. One boss told me, "Our staff just does not have the qualities that were there in the old days." (I did not tell him that an important part of what he actually meant by those "qualities" was the ability to work for low wages and let him make lots of money.) But when it comes to commitment and loyalty to their employees, employers often do not walk the talk. Employees fear the kind of experience that one man had during my executive training session at the University of Michigan's Executive Program. Upon returning from a break, he told me that he had just received a message that his firm had been bought out and that his severance package was on his desk! In this climate the question becomes whether or not the employee can trust the firm. This is something that too many employers fail to grasp. With so many buyouts, amalgamations, mergers, and consolidations, employees feel that whether or not they *want* to work at the same firm for a lifetime, they certainly are *unlikely* to do so. Hence, the view in the past used to be focused on positioning of assignments; now the focus is on the pedagogical and learning quality of assignments: "What can I learn that I can take with me?"

Employees' point of view has, therefore, changed from what it was in the past. They tend to side with Stan Davis and Jim Botkin's argument in *The Monster Under the Bed:* if you are not *learning* at your current job, move on![1] Things are changing too fast for you not to be always in training.

■ Problems

A number of problems beset both opportunity for advancement and opportunity for growth as organizations seek to craft these elements and make them an integral part of a sensible compensation system. I've already mentioned the issue of flattening organizations, which creates a reduced number of higher positions from the get-go. Correlatively, on the organizational learning side, it's true that firms spend lots of money today educating employees. But *educating* is probably the wrong word. Much of the so-called education budget is spent on training, some of it training that the employee should have received in a public or private school system, some of it specific to the organization. Some, of course, is spent on tuition at outside organizations— universities, degree programs, nondegree programs, and the like. The auto companies in Detroit, for example, are among the many firms that assist their employees in earning an MBA. One of the problems from the student's point of view, however, is that the firms in question don't always seem to have a good plan for using the acquired skills in any way that makes sense to the student. Hence the employee goes to school at night, finishes an MBA, and then winds up doing exactly the same job as before getting the degree. It's obviously nice to get a free MBA (not counting your own sweat equity), but organizations lose a lot when they spend hundreds of thousands of dollars on employee education and then fail to connect it to their own mission, vision, and values. More often than not, there is no career-pathing plan for the employee either.

As McClelland notes in *The Achievement Motive*,[2] individuals have four sets of motivational needs: need for achievement, need for power, need for affiliation, and need for autonomy. Need for autonomy and need for affiliation are dealt with in the next chapter in connection with the topics of job design and the work community. It is the first two—the so-called nAch and nPow—that are at issue here. The *nAch* variable characterizes the extent to which people wish to excel in a task. That is, individuals with high nAch have a need for personal excellence and constantly seek challenges, securing needed skills and feedback to help them better their personal best; those with low nAch prefer to keep things on an even keel and maintain their comfort level. The *nPow* variable characterizes the extent to which people like to run things for themselves or let others worry about running things (high nPow or low nPow). Organizations will have a difficult time separating need for achievement from need for power. People who want to be good at things are not the same as people who want to run things, but it takes some thought to develop valid and reliable company-specific ways for telling the difference. This problem is made a bit worse by a couple of confounding elements. First, there is an intersect here—people who want to be really good at running things. Second, looking at nPow alone, there are two faces of power, faces we all recognize. One is the more positive face of power, in which an individual seeks to lead out of a desire to make the enterprise go better. This is the person in the intersect. The negative face of power is displayed by the individual who seeks positions mainly for reasons of personal aggrandizement. As far as possible, employers need to discern which employees have which orientation, advance the former, and get rid of the latter. They're well-poisoners wherever they are.

Opportunity for Advancement

The first problem in the advancement area involves respinning the idea that all advancement is good. Individuals need resocialization to a new set of values in which cherished measures of success are not tied exclusively to higher positions in organizations, but instead embrace both nPow (advancement) and nAch (growth).

A second problem is promoting the right people. Regrettably, many firms are case studies in the Peter Principle.[3] Let me thumbnail the hypothesis: *The greater the degree of success you have in your current job, the more likely you are to be targeted for advancement, until you are advanced to a job where you cannot perform. There you will remain.* I'm sure many of us have observed the Peter Principle in action, as we have looked at a particular manager and wondered, "How could that turkey have gotten to that spot?" The answer was that the manager was good at the *last* job, which used skills the current spot doesn't require. Hence, preparation for advancement means preparation for the ability to use future skills rather than current skills. The fact that individuals are good at what they do should not automatically mean that they should stop doing it. Conversely, and perhaps this effort will be the more difficult, employers need to be open to the possibility that someone who is not particularly good at a current job should not necessarily be ruled out for a different and higher job. Not all good teachers make good principals, and some poor teachers make terrific principals.

A third issue is the need to assess the kind of ambition an employee has. Obviously, the ambition of the employee to get ahead is a factor. However, the one with the most ambition isn't necessarily the best suited for a higher hierarchical position. Therefore, firms need to look at whether individuals exhibit the proper face of power or are self-aggrandizers who will help only themselves. And some ambitious people really do not want to work as hard as the higher-level position requires to be successful at it.

Finally, firms need to get into the "flow" channel, depicted in Figure 7.1. This illustration suggests that systems (including both organizations and people) function best when they are at the intersection of challenge and skill—A_1 and A_3.[4] If skill exceeds challenge, then boredom (A_2) sets in; if challenge exceeds skill,

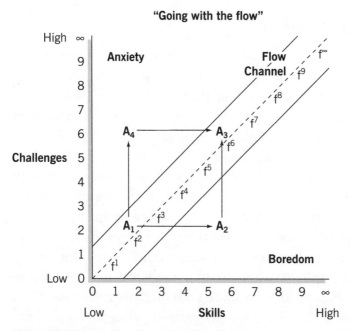

Figure 7.1. Why the Complexity of Consciousness Increases as a Result of Flow Experiences

Source: Adapted from Mihaly Csikszentmihalyi, *Flow: The Psychology of Optimal Experience* (New York: HarperCollins, 1991), p. 74.

then anxiety (A_4) sets in. Smart managers align their compensations in the flow channel. The goal is the challenge; the skills are the tools to get there. Whether an employee is heading for advancement or growth, or both, staying in the flow channel is critical. The point is that one cannot remain stable. The workplace is a dynamic setting. One has three choices of movement—up the channel, above the channel (anxiety), or below the channel (boredom). The default position seems to be downward drift. As employees get better at their jobs they require more challenge—but often they do not get it, and thus drift into boredom. The f's running up the flow channel represent increasingly complex (higher challenge, higher skill) functions that employees are performing. As one moves up the flow channel one develops a more complex consciousness—and hence better functioning.

Opportunity for Growth

With respect to opportunity for growth, one problem will be learning to view training and education as part of a compensation system, rather than as something that meets some manager's or employee's immediate need. Firms need to be more strategic and organized about the kinds of training and education that will make their enterprises successful. That will be, I think, a reach for most firms. It will be a reach because it requires firms to think through what kinds of education and training they wish to offer, and why. The conclusions of *that* thinking are what go into the package. Anything else becomes an "X" element in the total compensation equation, something that an individual employee wants for individual reasons. It is particularly important to identify those with high nAch, because those individuals will leave if the assignment package is not stimulating enough for them and they do not see themselves as improving at their craft.

A second problem concerns cost. Education and training are an investment in people. Many organizations—Alcoa, for one—have an internal "university" of their own. But connecting education and training to the bottom line is tough. Partly this is so because the costs of a failure to provide adequate education and training often appear elsewhere than in the training budget and are thus hidden. For example, if an employee leaves because of lack of training opportunities in the firm or better opportunities elsewhere, the costs appear in recruitment budgets and as replacement costs. Hence they are not connected with the education and training enterprise.

Third, education and training are vulnerable parts of the overall budget. Training, like travel, is still viewed as an extra rather than as an essential in many firms. Like music in the schools, it is among the first items to be cut.

■ Suggested Solutions

As firms move to include opportunities for advancement and, especially, growth in their overall operation, certain elements need to be taken into consideration.

Advancement

A good number of firms are already well into the advancement piece. They focus on selecting high-potential individuals and have begun to vary assignments and experiences throughout the firm to prepare selected recruits for higher-level responsibilities. However, many of these high-potential employees are never told what is happening; they can only surmise it based on firm lore. Hence the firm loses the enthusiastic participation of the employee.

Once identified, high-potential individuals need to be career pathed. I will call advancement-oriented career pathing *ladderpathing*. That means that specialists in the organization need to think through with these individuals what kinds of paths they would find useful, what kinds of experiences would work best for them, where their deficiencies are, and how their strengths might be exploited and enhanced. If employees and employers agree that advancement into management ranks is appropriate, then some training in management may be useful—to help prevent the new manager from becoming a "boss from hell" and perhaps even help him or her become a great boss.

The next step is to lay out a plan for assignments and challenges over a several-year period. That will help the individual prepare for steps that are laid out in the future. The more an employee knows about the likely path, the more possible it is for the person to prepare for the upcoming assignments. This preparation sometimes involves pre-positioning employees for upcoming assignments (for instance, a year in Brazil as preparation for a future job involving international responsibilities).

Finally, a mentor program for individuals as they move into a new position helps round out the plan. Once employees take on a new job, too often the message is "Hey, you're on your own." They don't have anyone with whom they can confer on a neutral basis who is off-line from their current supervisory structure.

Growth

With respect to opportunities for growth, activities fall into two basic parts. One has to do with latticepathing and the other with the firm's own education and training curriculum.

Latticepathing means working with each employee to develop a learning path within—and perhaps outside—the firm. Of particular importance is the development of technical tracks. Still, in many industrial settings, the way to get ahead is to move up in the management ranks. The career lattice is a response to this rigid practice. Some employees want to be better at their skill, not higher in the organization. And, of course, it makes sense to help employees become better at what they already do well, if that is their wish. Opportunities for growth are made real through a latticepath document, which specifies the kinds of experiences and training that the employee needs for personal development. On the assignments side, the firm must stand ready to make the specified types of assignments available.

This commitment to growth-oriented assignments is a kind of compensation. I know a business that tries to make this happen, but is so ham-handed that it winds up making people angry rather than happy. Here is an example. An employee asked for an international assignment. The people at the firm replied that that was a good idea, and they would see what they could do. Then they got back to the employee with the information that something would come up in a couple of years, but they would not say what it might be. Every so often the same message was repeated, but still all details—potential details, actually—were "confidential."

Over the two-year period, the man met and became engaged to the love of his life. One day his boss called him into the office and said, "You are going to our plant in Italy, within the month." Leaving aside the peremptory nature of the communication, which in itself is a problem, there was no inquiry about whether the employee's situation was still the same. The employee said that he was getting married and was not able to turn around on a dime, as he had been able to do in the past. The manager was angry, saying, "But you said you wanted to go overseas!" "That was two years ago," the employee replied. "Things change. If you had kept me in the loop, I could have given you a heads-up."

Here is a situation where the company was simply woodenheaded. I believe the people there thought, and still think, that they were upstanding and that the problem was an ungrateful employee. The take-away here is that, if you are planning assignments with an employee, plan *with* the employee, not, in private, *for* the employee.

Work-based experiential assignments are one piece of the latticepathing pie. The other piece is a series of educational and training experiences that fit into the employee's total career plan. Educational experiences may involve degrees (an MBA, for example) or special training programs at executive education programs. The plan may also involve training within the educational program of the firm itself, especially if it is a sizable one.

Firms also need to think through their own offerings. They then need to market the opportunity for growth as a positive factor in their workplace. Such opportunities can include not only in-house training but also support for outside training and education.

A firm's own curriculum can be organized around several categories of training and education. There is, obviously, the technical piece. That has to do with helping employees do the job they are currently doing, and most organizations of any size do a pretty good (or at least an enthusiastic) job of that.

A second component is team-based training and activities. Despite the growth of teams in business and industry, both in the United States and worldwide, team training represents a big gap in many firms' curricula. This is particularly true of certain aspects of work in teams, including effective group decision making, running effective meetings, and so on.

Most firms could also benefit from offering training in supportive communication. Time after time, when workers are asked what they don't like about their job, mainly they say their bosses, their colleagues and peers, and their subordinates—basically, everybody else at work. In other words, the main dissatisfier at work is the people at work. My own focus-group research suggests that it is not people in general that are the problem, but rather people who don't listen, who don't communicate well, who don't bring others into the loop, and so on. Hence communication training should be a priority, the more so when firms want to implement a team approach.

Finally, there are intrapersonal, interpersonal, and maturational programs. Ongoing training in self-awareness can help. Emotional intelligence, for example, has made a big impact in corporate America. Emotional intelligence refers to one's ability to recognize and manage feelings in self and other.[5] Daniel Goleman's books *Emotional Intelligence* and *Working with Emotional Intelligence* have attracted lots of attention.[6] His recent article in the *Harvard Business Review*, "Leadership That Gets Results," has added to the interest.[7] "EQ" is becoming as important to employers as the IQ, and many organizations are giving thought to doing some training in this area.

Training in emotional intelligence could be of great use to almost any employee. Like the other kinds of growth-oriented training, it represents a take-away for the employee, useful for the firm but portable with respect to the skills.

On occasion, though, general training is insufficient. Especially in the executive arena, a personal touch is needed. Some of the work I do as an executive coach concerns this subject. To a great extent, executives with whom I work are concerned with individuals who seem to be deeply clueless about how they affect the workplace. These executives frequently ask for my suggestions on ways to get through to individuals who seem to have no sense of how what they do affects others. The executives themselves, of course, are less forthcoming about their own cluelessness, and a sizable number of individuals with whom I've worked have been referred to me for exactly that syndrome. Sometimes I'm the one who has to provide the proverbial "whack on the side of the head." Most managers tell me that the people they have problems with are not in the doghouse because of lack of technical expertise. Rather, they are in trouble because of intrapersonal and interpersonal deficits that are hampering their career development. (For more information on coaching, check out the Executive Coaching and Resource Network.[8])

A second area of maturational skills has to do with stress management. The Changing Times Web site talks about it this way (and provides a stress test as well): "Stress is one of the principal causes of lost productivity, social breakdown and ill-health. It can be caused by adverse pressures at work or in social situations. This web site, published by Changing Times, provides an insight to the causes and effects of stress and offers a jargon-free understanding of the problems that arise from excessive levels of stress."[9] Programs for stress management and reduction are helpful to employer and employee.[10]

Closely related to stress management and reduction is the issue of time management. The Mind Tools Web site can help.[11] We can all relate to the fact that individuals waste a lot of time at work. Efficiency is one of the skills that most interest employers, and was a key principle in early scientific management studies. Time management programs have been among the more popular training programs that employers provide for employees.

Workplace health and wellness is an area of wide-ranging importance that takes in workplace safety, controlling substance abuse, smoking abatement programs, and personal fitness and wellness.[12] Employers are providing a number of programs in this area, from teaching about nutrition to personal fitness tests. Others go further and provide gyms and counselors as well. There is little question that healthy employees are more productive, and they reduce absenteeism and workers' comp costs. They can lower health benefits costs as well.

Maturational and personal training is not necessarily something that each organization has to provide on its own. Rather, it can be supportive of this area, and individuals can get the training from commercial vendors. Or there can be collaborative or collective educational enterprises within a particular community or region. The point is that these skill sets can indeed help the individual grow as a person while at the same time providing substantial benefits for the employer.

■ Concluding Suggestions

Organizations need to have growth ladders as well as hierarchical ladders. If you have an engineer who's a good engineer and wants to stay as an engineer, you need to provide technical ladders of knowledge and respect that parallel what used to be the only ladder in town, the corporate ladder.

But ladders need to be complemented by lattices. There are several things that an organization can do to provide compensation that includes both.

As an overall step, begin a program to assure yourself that each employee has both a ladderpath and a latticepath. Depending on your anticipated needs and employees' interests and performance, one or the other should be dominant for each individual. Assessment instruments for advancement or growth interests—need for achievement and need for power, for example, can be used.[13] That selection can be changed as time passes. A new Web site, hrgems.com, allows employers to make their own tests and store them on the site, along with results for each employee who takes the test. Employees take the tests on the Web and employers can work with updated information.

With respect to opportunities for advancement, assess your own shop to ascertain what you are already doing in terms of advancement programs, especially for employees and new recruits judged to have high potential. Here, as in the other areas, building a way to get regular employee input into the kinds of things they would like to have available is invaluable.

With respect to opportunities for growth, a good first step is to read *The Monster Under the Bed* by Davis and Botkin to get a better sense of what is needed in today's market. Their argument is that employees should always be learning on the job and through the job while doing the job. Here, too, asking employees for input is always a positive move.

Second, see whether there are ways to focus and structure educational programs for better return for the employee and the firm. In particular, look strategically at the kinds of education and training that you currently offer, and ask why you do what you do. Many of the programs can leverage employer interests. Health and wellness programs, for example, benefit both employer and employee in specific ways.

Third, tally the costs of both in-house and outside education and training. Consider ways in which the total education and training program might be more smoothly connected to both employee wishes and business strategy. Avoid putting yourself in the position of the firms that support MBA training but have no real plan for what to do with the freshly minted MBA after graduation.

Finally, establish—and reward—technical growth as well as hierarchical advancement. We all know that not every teacher wants to be a principal; some want to be better and more challenging teachers. Let's help them achieve that goal.

CHAPTER SUMMARY

In today's business world, "getting ahead" means something a bit different from what it meant in the past. Previously, higher in the organization was the only established goal, and the faster one climbed the better it was. Today, however, the career ladder has been supplemented—which is not to say supplanted—by the career lattice. Firms need to distinguish between opportunities for advancement and opportunities for growth, and then provide for both.

Part of the message here, as with other chapters in this book, is that opportunities for advancement and growth need to be considered part of overall compensation and integrated with the compensation program. This is not only a matter of administration, it is also a matter of aligning these opportunities with the overall mission, values, and goals of the organization. The need for such alignment is all the greater in a time of flatter organizations and new employee expectations. A further implication is that job-related knowledge needs to be conceptualized in a way that encompasses more than specific skills related to an employee's current position. Firms need to support the development of portable skills that enhance employees' value both along the organizational lattice and up the organizational ladder.

The Softer Side of Compensation

Psychic Income, Quality of Life, and the *X* Factor

M oney has become such a powerful factor in American society that it often defines our very selves. We have come to believe that "richer is better." Of course money is important, so important that rich people often worry about how to use it, as Father John Haughey discusses in his book *The Holy Use of Money*.[1] The problem for the compensation specialist is that money is not *all* that is important, and the other things that matter must not be ignored.

Even our aphorisms tell this story. "It's the money, stupid" tells a part of the story, but "Money can't buy everything" tells another important part. In one study, done in 1981, students ranked "money" ninth of eighteen factors that they looked at in thinking about a job.[2] I mention the year because even twenty years ago there was a sense of importance of other factors. These other factors are becoming more heavily weighted with a new generation of workers, but this new generation is building on something that was already present though largely ignored in the worker mind-set.

Sandy Jencks and his colleagues looked at this question from a sociological perspective a few years later, in 1988. They developed an Index of Job Desirability, which included the factors shown in Table 8.1, among others.[3] Earnings are the most important element in a job's desirability; however, thirteen *nonmonetary* job characteristics are, taken together, twice as important as money.[4] The numbers (beta weights) are a statistical measure of how important each variable is in comparison to the others. A minus sign means that the variable has a negative value. Hence, jobs that get you dirty at work, have frequent

Table 8.1. Beta Weights for Selected Variables in Index of Job Desirability

Rank	Variable	Beta Weight
01	Earnings	.214
02	Educational requirement (more required)	.165
03	Hours greater than 35	.145
04	On-the-job training	.134
05	Gets dirty at work	−.132
06	Vacation weeks (has more)	.107
07	Decides own hours	.106
08	Frequent supervision	−.104
09	Union contract (has one)	.099
10	Proportion repetitive	−.096
11	Federal employee	.090
12	State employee	−.071
13	Boss has boss	−.082
14	Risk of job loss	−.082

Source: Christopher Jencks, Lauri Perman, and Lee Rainwater, "What Is a Good Job? A New Indicator of Labor Market Success," *American Journal of Sociology* 93, no. 6 (May 1988): 1336.

supervision (micromanaging), or are repetitive are negatives. Working for a state government is also negative, as are being at risk of losing your job and being down in the hierarchy ("boss has boss").

It seems clear, then, that there are many features of the workplace that make a job more (or less) desirable besides the paycheck. Work is a source of meaning (positive or negative) as well as money. It is also a community within which workers interact and one they share with other communities in which they participate, such as ethnic and geographic communities. And in many cases work contains that extra element, which I term the X factor, that adds a bit of zest and makes life even more worthwhile.

Barbara Parus of WorldatWork (formerly the American Compensation Association) points to these kinds of things. She talks about "building a company of owners."[5] Part of the idea of a company of owners is, of course, that workers have a financial stake in the firm. But there are other pieces, which she passes along from Bill Shannon of William M. Mercer. They include items discussed in this and earlier chapters:

- *Meaningful work:* Employees have challenging and significant work.
- *Business information:* Employees have a solid understanding of the business and ongoing access to relevant information.
- *Leadership:* Top leadership is fully committed.
- *Employee involvement:* Employees make meaningful decisions or have input into significant decisions.
- *Performance feedback:* Employees get ongoing feedback from multiple sources on their contribution to the business.
- *Career management:* The company makes a long-term commitment to employee career growth.

Most of this package is included in the last three terms of the total compensation equation. *Psychic income* addresses the emotional rewards (or disappointments) of the workplace, with particular reference to the work itself and interaction with other people—subordinates, peers, and superiors. *Quality of life* asks about the relationship of worklife to whole life. This issue is often thought of as the work-family balance in particular jobs, but it also includes the way in which life and job mesh. For example, commuting time and the physical location of the workplace are issues. *The X factor* refers to particular things that specific individuals may need and want, but also to the fact that Gen X and other cohorts of workers are redefining workplace expectations and behaviors in, I think, positive ways.

■ Psychic Income: The Best Things in Life Are Free

Psychic income is that set of properties of job, work, and workplace that create emotional satisfaction. It is that match between personal motivation and values and the workplace—the job situation, the work, the boss, and the workplace community—that creates an enhanced sense of satisfaction and personal pleasure. Employers could work on each of these areas to gain commitment and effort from workers. Ignoring psychic income has these damaging consequences:

- You have to pay much more to get people to come and to stay.
- You are continually worried about people skimming the system, working the system, or ripping off the system.
- Empowerment is down; people are not really paying attention; errors and rework become the norm.

The Problems

A fundamental problem in the area of psychic income is that employers talk about things like morale but really pay very little structured attention to them. This means that there is wasted potential in the system, win-win opportunities that go begging. Mostly, I think, this is because, lacking a total compensation structure, employers do not know what to offer and employees don't know what to ask for, or are hesitant to ask if they do know.

It is also true that some of the elements required to provide positive psychic income at the workplace may seem too "soft." Or, more profoundly, they may challenge the ways in which firms are organized. For example, employees like work better when they can do a whole job, or a whole segment of a job, that is, when they have what is called "task identity." But some elements of creating a job with task identity involve rethinking, at least in part, structures and concepts like the "assembly line" and "division of labor." The result of too much division of the work is that no employee has a sense of the whole. In fact, excessive division of labor robs employees of one of the most important rewards that can be derived from work, a phenomenon Karl Marx called "exploitation."

Such sources of resistance are about to change. The question for contemporary firms is whether they can reinvent themselves quickly enough to provide this part of the rewards program.

A second problem is the work itself. Work is the larger context of the job. For an electrician, wiring may be the job, but the *work* is helping individuals in homes and businesses get the power they need. One likes to feel that one's work has a larger social value. As a student in a joint master's program in business administration and social work put it, "My job—my work, really—has to give me more than money. I need a sense of personal fulfillment."

John Calvin articulated the concept of the *calling*, the idea that each individual was called by God to do a particular task. This notion made every task God's task. That certainly raised the ante in taking out the garbage![6] Some people—relief workers, clergy, social workers, teachers, doctors—sacrifice a lot of base pay for the psychic income of helping others (well, not all doctors). By the same token, work that subtracts from the common health and welfare—delivering cigarettes to a 7-Eleven store, say—has a built-in negative psychic income. Where they can, which is in most cases, employers may want to consider emphasizing the larger social value of their products and services, thus enhancing the value of the work.

A third area of problems is the boss. This probably means you. If there is any doubt about the negative power of bad bosses, it should be dispelled by the transcendent popularity of the "Dilbert" series by Scott Adams.[7] The pointy-haired boss, dumb as a stone, seems to have become an emblem for many, if not most, bosses. From my perspective, bad bosses—from the clueless to the malevolent to the psychotic—cause untold human misery at the workplace. Further, abusive bosses cause employees to leave.[8] As Amy Zipkin reported in the *New York Times*, "A Gallup Organization study shows that most workers rate having a caring boss even higher than they value money or fringe benefits. In interviews with two million employees at 700 companies Gallup found that how long an employee stays at a company, and how productive she is there, is determined by her relationship with her immediate supervisor. 'People join companies and leave managers,' said Marcus Buckingham, a senior managing consultant at Gallup and the primary analyst for the study."[9]

Additional analyses from Spherion and Lou Harris found that "employees with the worst bosses were the most likely to leave." Of their interviewees, fully 40 percent of those who gave their bosses poor grades said they were looking for a new job, compared to only 11 percent of those who gave their boss an excellent rating.[10]

To these grim findings we can add the following: a 1999 Hudson Institute study of 2,293 employees found that 56 percent said their company did not genuinely care about them or their careers, and 55 percent—virtually the same proportion—

said they didn't have a strong loyalty to the company.[11] The role of poor management in creating negative psychic income and driving employees away is one of the most powerful factors in "anti-retention" of employees.

I think you can see the source of the problem here. Not only does attention to psychic income threaten existing structures and cultures, it threatens existing managers, the very people who are supposed to implement new compensation plans. On top of *that*, such implementation requires them to acknowledge that their own performance may be substantially lacking. I am not holding my breath.

Things actually get worse. The last problem is the workplace community—the other employees. There are two aspects to this concern. One is working to create a supportive environment among and within employee groups, a positive workplace community where other employees are pleasant and positive. The other is perhaps more difficult. It involves working to create what one of my friends calls a "jerk-free" environment.[12] This means addressing rather than ignoring issues of problematic and toxic employees in the workplace. People get furious when they play more or less by the rules, while someone who chronically abuses them seems to have immunity. Even more serious is the well-poisoner, who destroys the quality of the workplace through tactics such as bullying, displays of bad attitude, constant complaining, sabotage, character assassination, sexual harassment, emotional outbursts, and theft of office supplies. Former Indiana University basketball coach Bobby Knight has become an emblem of the emotional and physical bully, apparently intimidating colleagues, subordinates, and perhaps superiors for years. Prior to his firing, his workplace would not have qualified as "jerk-free." Perhaps it was her experience with this kind of setting that led Evelyn, founder of the Red Hot Law Group, to begin the "NAP"—No Assholes Policy—a feature of the firm.[13]

Suggested Solutions

Solutions for the issues of psychic income are difficult because they require active, indeed proactive, management. It is so much easier to give someone a few bucks than to actually improve the system. Yet there is huge upside potential if employers would look carefully at the following areas:

The Job
Job performance potential and job design are the two areas that can make a great difference here. A "great job" is one that allows for outstanding performance—or what is often called "peak performance," or working in the "flow channel." The general definition of flow experience offered in Chapter Seven is that it is at the intersection of skill and challenge. Now we are in a position to expand a bit on this definition. Consider the following equation:

$$\text{High Performance} = \text{Ability} \times \text{Motivation}$$

This equation means that, if the highest measure for ability and motivation are each 10, then a "10–10" employee would have a score of 100. A "5–10" or "10–5" employee would have a score of 50. We can make the equation more useful, though, by analyzing the terms:

$$\text{Ability} = \text{Aptitude} \times \text{Training} \times \text{Resources}$$
$$\text{Motivation} = \text{Desire} \times \text{Commitment}$$

This breakdown means that employers have five variables to work with in helping employees to perform: locating people with aptitude, providing training, supplying resources, enhancing desire, and building commitment. All of these things are what coaches do. Hence the "manager as coach" idea is not far off the mark. Working with these variables means that the employer is helping the employee to high performance, which the employee loves (don't we all love to do things well?) and which directly and indirectly benefits the employer.

One might ask, however, "performance at what?" The answer, of course, is the job, which brings us to a second area that employers can improve: job design. Good jobs have the following motivating features:[14]

- *Skill variety:* A chance to use different skills in the skill set
- *Task identity:* A chance to do the whole task
- *Knowledge of results:* A chance to know what happened as a result of your work
- *Experienced meaningfulness:* A chance to "feel" what happened as a result of your work
- *Autonomy:* A chance to do it your way, within some limits
- *Experienced responsibility:* A chance to be accountable for your actions
- *Feedback:* Information on how your performance is going

Jobs that are high on these elements have high psychic income. Employers should look to see whether the jobs in their organization meet the criteria discussed here in terms of job performance potential and job design.

Firms need to offer opportunities for high performance by assisting in ability and motivation development and by enhancing job design. These are "compensables" that firms can offer to employees. But there is one more point. Everyone needs to have some recognition of doing a good job. This means a recognition program that is appropriate, updated, varied, and sincere. The value of a $20,000 award is less if you are told, "Don't tell anyone!" By the same token, a $1,000 award, presented with a little hoopla and celebration, may actually go much further.

The Work

Employers need to develop ways to enhance the dignity and satisfaction associated with the work employees do. Titles that emphasize the service that employees provide are one way to enhance the meaning in work. Granted, changing someone's title from "salesperson" to "customer fulfillment specialist" can sound like so much hokum. And often it is. But the underlying point is very solid, particularly if the job itself is designed to live up to the title. "Garbage collector" sounds, well, yucky; "sanitation worker" sounds better, partly because it emphasizes the service being performed instead of the crummy aspect of the job. And, in spite of all the bad press that garbage collectors get, theirs is an absolutely essential line of work. The same is true of aides in nursing homes. It is not just a question of job title but of the way workers are treated and socialized to think of themselves and their work. So often I have heard people say, "I would never want *that* job." Exactly who, I wonder, do they think will care for them when they need care? It is an absolutely vital job, to the patient and to the society, one that deserves honor and respect. Providing honor and respect can start anywhere, of course, but right at the nursing home is a good place to begin.

Good Managers and Management

This is one of the two real toughies. (The workplace community, discussed next, is the other.) It is essential to offer supportive leadership and management. Yet the managers who need to do this are often themselves dumber than stones, or at least lacking in self-reflection and awareness. For this reason, this is a great place to employ organizational climate surveys done by an outside firm.

To be a good manager you need to do good—*and* not do bad. These are not the opposite of each other. Rather, they are orthogonal. Imagine drawing two lines, intersecting as in a plus sign. The horizontal line represents "doing bad," while the vertical line represents "doing good." Each line is divided into ten segments, 0–9. A 9 means you get a high score on the vector. At the extremes, one can be a "9–9" manager—doing lots good *and* lots bad—or a "1–1" manager, who doesn't do much of anything. To be an excellent manager, you have to do a lot right and very little wrong. Doing right means assisting employees, providing resources to them, being a mentor to them, and being interested in their careers as well as your own. Amy Zipkin's *New York Times* article, cited a few pages back, says it better than anything. The thousands of books on management should tell us something about the high interest in this area. The problem seems to be that "interest" in managing well, as is true of other areas with thousands of resources such as losing weight and being fit, has not been translated into the actuality. Doing bad is even more complicated. Since pernicious managers are unlikely to reform themselves, I will mention them in discussing the workplace community, our next topic.

The Workplace Community

Because the workplace is a community—a schoolyard, as it were—its members have to work and play well together. Employees flourish if there is a set of shared values in the workplace. Communities flourish if they are suffused with honesty, loyalty, kindness, self-control, and cooperation. They are harmed by vices like lying, cruelty, treachery, self-indulgence, laziness, uncontrolled aggressiveness, and selfishness.[15] Now, doesn't that sound like the difference between a great place to work and a rotten, toxic one? The problem is that in today's world, and in tomorrow's even more so, workers are looking for the great workplaces, and leaving the rotten ones.

One source of rottenness in a workplace is, as I have said, the manager. Managers are, among other things, leaders of the workplace community. This means that, as part of the compensation system for workers, successful organizations are going to have to weed out the awful managers and train ordinary managers to be extraordinary. Further, managers will have to intervene in the schoolyard, as it were, by weeding out those individuals who are not working and playing well together. They cannot go on letting the workplace be spoiled by employees who lie or who are cruel, disloyal, self-indulgent, lazy, dangerously aggressive, or selfish.

As a practical matter, firms can offer several things to employees as a way to bring this area of compensation to life:

- *Regular climate surveys:* When employees know that the firm regularly asks them about the climate of the workplace community, that is a plus. The chance to reflect on both system practices and individual behaviors should be part of the survey.
- *Regular surveys on managers:* When an employee knows that the manager gets a 360-degree evaluation, that is a plus.[16]
- *One-on-ones:* One-on-one sessions, which can occur in a meeting or through managing-by-wandering-around, are one means of finding out about toxic individuals and the ways in which their behavior is destructive.
- *Know it—do it:* Having the information is one thing; acting on it is another thing. As part of your recruitment, invite new recruits to meet old recruits (current employees). They will pass the word that *this* workplace has a "find and fix" mind-set.
- *Boss choice:* Boss choice is somewhat like school choice, and it is an option that is consistent with the cafeteria compensation system. The idea is, "If you do not like your boss, you can choose another one." We use that system for student advisers at the University of Michigan. I know that it seems, at first, a bit on the odd side. But the message it conveys is a powerful one. And, as with school choice, if everyone flees one particular boss, there is a powerful message there as well.

■ Quality of Life

Quality of life (QL) deals essentially with achieving a work-life/whole-life balance, and having the health to enjoy both.[17] How, for example, does one's worklife fit into one's whole life? Or, as the *Wall Street Journal's* Sue Shellenbarger titled one of her columns, "What Job Candidates Really Want to Know: Will I Have a Life?"[18] Since one big part of life is family, quality of life comes to focus a lot on work-family issues. Another part of the QL package, though, is worker health, both physical and mental. It is hard to have balance between work and family if the employee is sick.

The Problems

There are many problems in the quality of life area. For purposes of this book, I would like to focus on that package of issues that are called, loosely, *worklife/homelife balance.*

Worklife/homelife balance problems reflect a cultural change over the last fifty to one hundred years. With industrialization, people moved from the family farm, where everybody worked and took care of all the details of home life, to workplaces where work went on separately from family concerns. Long hours "at work" became the norm. Whyte's *The Organization Man* told the story well.[19] Today, jobs are done by a diverse range of people, women especially, for whom older models of six in the morning to six in the evening do not fit. Three "G" forces are pushing change: generational (Gen X), global (worldwide competition), and gender (women in the labor force). To these forces, which continue to operate, we can add the Internet, which is having its own huge impact, in part because it allows access to information about what other organizations are doing. Employees realize that their workplace does not have to be the bad place it sometimes is; other workplaces are different! And the employees learn techniques for change from other employees who have been successful in changing their own workplaces to better, healthier communities. So one problem is to find ways to make the workplace—hours and locations—more flexible.

A second problem is that achieving balance among life interests has become a key need—one that is shared by many young employees. Old-style employers often think they can schedule plant and office operations with complete disregard for the lives of the employees. As one young engineer complained, "Our management, and I use that term with utter scorn, has decided that we will have one-hour meetings at eight and four every Saturday and Sunday for the foreseeable future. We are all outraged. And we never do anything at the meetings. It is abuse, pure and simple." Another thirty-something engineer said, "I want a job and a family too. My boss is at the plant day and night; he never sees his three kids that I can see. It's just not the way I want to live my life. But I feel I am trapped in it, we are all trapped in it, because he expects us to work like he does." The challenge, then, is to achieve greater harmony between home and work schedules.

A third problem is overwork. All this work can get to you. We hear from Juli Schorr about the "overworked American."[20] And it may be true. Everyone seems really busy. This leads to problems like "the second shift" that Arlie Hochschild talks about,[21] in which so many women have a whole second job to do at home after they get off work. Companies have tried to be "family friendly," again as Hochschild detailed in *The Time Bind*.[22] But family friendly did not last very long, even at a very determined company.

These are not the only issues that affect worklife/homelife balance. There is the journey to work: How long is it? There is the physical location of the workplace: Is it pleasant and inviting? And I will mention workplace wellness again. It is hard to overstate the drain on QL that sickness brings. Companies need to think creatively about these issues.

Suggested Solutions

From a total compensation point of view we can consider suggested solutions for quality of life issues in three large groups. One has to do with company policy and recognition at the top of the organization that "QL" matters, no less than QA (quality assurance) and TQM (Total Quality Management). Compensation executives cannot relocate the plant. That is a job for the boardroom. Obviously, safety programs and workplace-wide programs (such as smoke-free policies) need to come from the higher-ups as well. But compensation executives need to market the importance of these items to other senior managers.

The second group has to do with educating the managers. Individual managers who schedule 8 A.M. meetings every Saturday need education. Without educated and committed managers the new programs will not work.

The third group of solutions comprises those programs that compensation managers need to put in place. Workplace wellness programs, for example, represent a proactive stance by employers toward health promotion. They involve newsletters devoted to health and safety, training and programs (such as smoking abatement and weight-loss programs, or access to counseling), and healthful cafeteria food. They provide both practical and useful interventions while communicating a caring posture on the part of the firm. They may well help the firm's bottom line as well, in the form of lower workers' compensation premiums and fewer sick days lost.

Worklife balance programs provide time and flexibility. Once "goodies," they are rapidly becoming necessities that firms are integrating into their organizational thinking. The key seems to be control over time. Now, obviously, firms are not going to say, "Come and go when you like, and we will still pay you." But wait a minute; why not? This question highlights the difference between the 9–5 mentality and a facetime measurement system on one hand and a flextime mentality and results-based measurement system on the other. As I noted in connection with high performance, employees *want* to do a good job. Employers need to give them the power to organize ways to get the job done, both with each other and with their own and each other's families. In this approach, span of control gives way (and it is so hard to give up!) to span of communication. *Boss* becomes *coach* and *mentor*. Bosses who help employees solve issues that employees are worried about free the employees for work.

There are many kinds of worklife programs, from child care to sabbaticals, from elder care to concierge services. Any or all may be appropriate in a particular firm. What underlies each of these programs is added flexibility for the employee. Someone once said that being an employee today is like driving a two-ton truck filled with three tons of canaries. To be successful it is necessary that one ton of canaries be in the air at all times.

The bottom line is that a good place to start with workplace programs is to move to a flextime environment. As always, ask your employees how to configure it, and then communicate it, over and over. A program buried in the policy book is no program at all.

There are other ways to give time as well. One increasingly popular idea is the much-maligned academic practice of the sabbatical. According to the *Wall Street Journal*, "Nearly half of Fortune's 100 Best Companies to Work for in America, in fact, now provide sabbaticals or similar leave programs—up 18% from just a year ago."[23]

■ The *X* Factor

We come to the final term in the total compensation equation, the X factor. It turns out that it really should be X^2 because, as we shall see, "X" has two meanings.

The Problems

In one of its meanings the X factor refers to Gen X. I have mentioned some of this group's special needs in Chapter One. I want to add a bit of detail here.

Gen X workers have some specific axes to grind with respect to the organization of many workplaces today. Their views reflect many of the points I have stressed throughout this volume. The following list of "things managers do that drive younger employees crazy," taken from Claire Rains's *Beyond Generation X*, makes the point clearly:

- They give raises that are virtually meaningless.
- They give insincere, gratuitous "thank you's" and pats on the back.
- They throw people into jobs they are not trained or qualified to do.
- They allow the workplace to be disorganized, cluttered, or dirty.
- They answer questions with "Because I said so" or an attitude like it.
- They overlook unacceptable behavior from staff members.
- They ignore employee opinions and ideas.
- They fail to give feedback and regular performance reviews.
- They micromanage.[24]

To be forewarned is to be forearmed. To recruit and retain Gen Xers it is necessary to consider factors that they consider important.

But "X" has another meaning here as well. In algebra, x is usually used for the unknown: "Solve for x." In the total compensation equation, X refers to the unique, individual things that might make the recruitment and retention difference to particular employees. One organization, for example, had to move someone's wine cellar. Another organization had to allow one new employee to begin employment with a "vacation" that he had scheduled with his wife before the move; another had to help the recruit's kid with a college reference and summer job. Yet another organization had to allow an employee's dog to come in to work with her. More traditional organizations would have lost these people. The idea here is to be open to those things employees might want that could make a difference for them, personally, and do it, if possible. Remember that one size does not fit all.

Suggested Solutions: Gen X

The things managers can do to attract and retain Gen Xers are consistent with good management practice. Here is the list I presented earlier of "things managers do that drive younger employees crazy," with an addition—what employers can do to earn the love of Gen X employees:

- *They give raises that are virtually meaningless.* Develop a sensible, accomplishment-based compensation system.
- *They give insincere, gratuitous "thank you's" and pats on the back.* Revisit "Attaboys" and "Attagirls." Pay attention to accomplishments and celebrate them appropriately.
- *They throw people into jobs they are not trained or qualified to do.* In a good compensation system, one that allows for opportunity for growth and employee choice, skill will be provided before or with challenge.

- *They allow the workplace to be disorganized, cluttered, or dirty.* Clean up the workplace!
- *They answer questions with "Because I said so" or an attitude like it.* Invite employees to develop their own solutions to problems. What matters is not your authority but the results.
- *They overlook unacceptable behavior from staff members.* Tank the toxics; junk the jerks!
- *They ignore employee opinions and ideas.* Develop regular systems for securing, and implementing, employee suggestions. After all, the ones who do the job know the job.
- *They fail to give feedback and regular performance reviews.* Implement regular performance reviews. Follow the rules of good feedback (see Chapter Four).
- *They micromanage.* Step back from "span of control"; change to span of communication.

Suggested Solutions for the "Mystery" X

When I talk with managers about the X factor, many become somewhat negative. "If I don't know what people want, how can I proceed?" they ask with irritation. That question comes out of the reactive compensation posture, the one that goes, "We give you this; if you want anything different, come and demand it and you probably will not get it." The mystery X implies a proactive compensation manager who is not only responding to but generating requests.

Being proactive means asking employees if there are things they need or would like that could make their workplace better for them. Taking the initiative is a form of compensation in and of itself. There are lots of things that might make an employee's life better that the firm *could* provide if only it knew about them. "Who knew?" is not the question you want to ask after the employee leaves.

If you leave it to them to speak up, many employees will be hesitant to ask for things they need or want, especially when a request crosses conventional lines of power (hierarchy, class, race, gender, and so on). Forcing people to ask can defeat the purpose of having an X element in the compensation equation. Bob Nelson's book *1001 Ways to Reward Employees* has become a classic set of suggestions for special things that employers can do for employees.[25]

When requests do come up, the compensation manager should not ask "Why?" but rather "Why not?" Of course, not every special need can be met. But the orientation I am advocating here—the positive, can-do perspective—is much different from the "can't do" perspective that characterizes many organizations.

In sum, these suggested solutions amount to adopting a positive attitude toward helping the employee out if possible, and providing the gift of invitation.

■ Concluding Suggestions

As with the other elements of the total compensation equation, the place to begin with the three elements discussed in this chapter is with an inventory of what you are doing now. The following lists outline the main points in this chapter. Take a look at them with some care. Then think about the questions that follow.

Psychic Income
- Appreciation of the employee's contribution
- Interesting job
- Meaningful work
- Decent bosses
- Jerk-free workplace community

Quality of Life
- Workplace wellness
- Worklife/homelife balance. (You might wish to review the Public Administration discussion on worklife.[26] It focuses on the federal government, but the application is really to us all—every sector must deal with the changing workforce, worklife balance, human capital, and program evaluation and management.)

The X Factor
- Gen X issues
- That special something

The basic question to ask about these topics is this: What kinds of efforts are we making, if any, in each of these areas? I will call things that are positive *positrons* and things that are negative *negatrons*. Ask yourself the following specific questions:

- How do I know what we *are* doing?
- Are there some positrons going on that are the result of individual managers pushing ahead?
- Are there some managers who are creating negatrons?
- If I were to give one point for each of the programs we have in these areas, what would my score be? What do I want it to be?
- Do I have a way of getting to employees on a regular basis and asking them what they need and want so that I can build programs from their input?
- Could I appoint someone on my staff to oversee these areas as a part of their job and really get these organized into sensible offerings?

As a further aid to taking inventory, consult the Winter 1998 special issue of the *ACA Journal*, published by the American

Compensation Association (now WorldatWork). Titled *The New Workplace: Balancing Work and Life Issues,* the issue has four sections—"Innovations," "Flexible Work Arrangements," "Wellness and Career Counseling," and "Family Care"—with a range of articles in each. Use the articles in the journal to identify ideas your firm might want to explore. Is your organization pushing the envelope on these aspects of compensation? Why or why not? How would you decide whether to proceed with some of the ideas you uncover?

CHAPTER SUMMARY

Psychic income, quality of life, and the *X* factor: these are the final elements of the total compensation equation. To attract and retain employees in today's marketplace, firms will need to look at providing psychic income, including factors such as an interesting job, meaningful work, decent bosses, and a nontoxic workplace. Quality of life is an important element as well, involving a healthy workplace and a balance of worklife and whole life. Finally, the *X* factor means attending to both the values of Gen Xers and the unknown *X* that any employee may need workplace help to manage.

Employers may or may not already be doing something about one or more of these areas, in a more or less deliberate and coordinated way. The chances are high that they are not doing enough, and not coordinating what different people are doing. Equally important for our purposes, whatever they are doing is probably being done under some rubric other than compensation. Yet these elements of the total compensation equation are highly salient to today's employees. They are a reason to work at one place rather than another. They are as truly compensation as cash is, and often at least as important.

PART 3

Changing the Old Pay Mind-Set and Structure

C hange! It seems so necessary, and yet so hard. There are all kinds of sayings about change: You have to change to stay the same; he who hesitates is lost; leadership is the ability to initiate and sustain change without crisis; if it ain't broke, don't fix it; if it ain't broke, break it!

While sayings like these reflect our recognition of the pressure for continual change, change has several properties that make us resist. One is that it takes us out of our comfort zone. That is unsettling, and causes us to work harder. A second is uncertainty: good results are never guaranteed. A third is that change is the great destroyer. It destroys old investments, commitments, and patterns. From a distance, the bad old days look like the good old days.

Compensation, with its unique fusion of practical and symbolic value, is perhaps the area in most firms that is most insulated from change. Almost every process, from increasing production efficiency and quality to running effective meetings, has been under the developmental gun. But compensation remains largely underconceptualized and out of alignment.

The spate of recent books on compensation is a harbinger of things to come. (A recent check of Amazon.com under "compensation" surfaced over two thousand titles!) The change in the name of the American Compensation Association to Worldat-Work is another signal. The wagon train of change is about to depart. This volume provides a destination.

Two kinds of change are needed. One is mind-set. Thinking about the positive aspects of changes—the benefits of the newer and better—is a key piece. The other is change in the "comp and benefits" areas—reorganizing the organization chart, providing new training and new responsibilities to employees (the compensation managers), and bringing all the parts of the compensation equation into a single organizational department or area. It sounds daunting. But, as I said in Chapter One, we have, in some ways, "been there, done that" with cafeteria benefits. So the transition to cafeteria compensation may not be as daunting as it seems.

The final chapter, on upgrading conventional compensation, is about the process of change. One helpful hint is in the title: upgrading (to first class!) is *good* change. Why not start with that perspective?

Upgrading Conventional Compensation

U pgrading—that is, changing—a compensation system is a Sisyphian task. Sisyphus, you will remember, was the ancient hero who was sentenced by the gods to roll a stone up a hill, and each night it rolled back down. Organizational change is a bit like that. You make some changes day by day, and suddenly at the end of the week it seems like it's the old system all over again. This resurrection of the old organization is something that Rosabeth Moss Kanter called "the ghost in the machine." It means that, even after the old organization has been replaced with a new one, the old one remains, slowly fading like an old ember. At times, a simple breath of air can bring it back to life.

□

Compensation system upgrade is, perhaps, the most challenging of all areas of organizational change because compensation is among the most value-rich areas in the firm. Money is, after all, money. It buys things. But as I have mentioned repeatedly, money is more than money, it is meaning, too: self-esteem, recognition, perhaps (in some contexts) a sign of God's favor. Mess with that at your peril. Nonetheless, mess we must. The old compensation system is the ghost in the machine. Without changes there, other changes fade away and older forms of behavior return. Change it along with—or better, ahead of—other changes and it becomes a beacon, a signal for direction rather than an anchor.

■ The Ultimate Destination: A Total Compensation Department

The logic of the total compensation approach suggests that the most desirable change would be to create a total compensation policy. Such a policy is written, it spells out the compensation choices available, and it is approved by legitimate authority. It is the document that reflects the firm's decision making with respect to its total compensation package (such a statement may already have been formulated for the cafeteria benefits program).

With the policy in place, the next step would be to create a Total Compensation Department. This department would contain the old functions of compensation, benefits, training, perks, various kinds of special arrangements that might be made for individuals ("X"), and so on. It would create one-stop shopping for compensation in the organization. It would be a place where employees could go to discuss their compensation interests— what they really want from the job—and have one individual who would be able to be the "problem owner" of a particular employee's compensation issue.

The cafeteria compensation notion is built on the idea of compensation choice or customization. It promotes a compensation policy that allows employees to do some configuring of their compensation package. Compensation case managers would assist employees in thinking through their package, and connect them to specialists in individual areas if necessary. The case manager would make every effort to address or configure an employee's compensation concerns or explain why the package could not be configured the way the employee wished, if that was the way it turned out.

Furthermore, each compensation case manager would keep a running record of requests, issues addressed and unaddressed, jobs completed and still incomplete, and so on. As a result, the case managers would be able to have periodic input into ways the system might be upgraded.

Such a thoroughgoing change in the way compensation is handled would be a transformational change, or upgrade—a change *of* the system. Sometimes, of course, such revolutionary change can't be accomplished. For a variety of reasons, it may be impractical to change the system as a whole. In such cases, evolution—that is, transactional change—might be a preferred strategy. Throughout this book, I have suggested specific solutions to compensation problems that can be part of such transactional change. These suggestions arose naturally in the context of the ongoing discussion of each part of the compensation equation. Now I would like to ratchet up the discussion to look at the process of change, the choices of change approaches, and the costs of change as a topic in its own right.

I'll begin by considering the choice between transformational and transactional upgrade of the compensation system. Then I'll discuss the issues that arise with either form of organizational change and offer some solutions.

□

■ Transformational Versus Transactional Upgrade

Both transformational (revolutionary) and transactional (evolutionary) change have advantages and disadvantages.[1] Let's consider the pros and cons of transformational upgrade first.

Transformational Upgrade

Big, sweeping change has a lot going for it. For one thing, it prunes away years of infrastructure, all those organizational thorns and brambles that keep catching the organization and preventing it from moving forward. The transformational upgrade requires everybody to go along; there simply isn't any alternative. You might or might not like it, but the train's leaving the station, and you're either on it or not. Again, if you're not part of the solution, you're part of the problem. Perhaps more concretely, you are either on the new train or taking some other form of transportation. If you cannot be part of the solution, then it is probably not the place you want to work. When a cafeteria benefits system, for example, gets rolled out, then everyone is on the plan.

A big upgrade in the compensation plan also means that the compensation concept moves from laggard to lead as a competitive piece in the organization. Organizations can be competitive on many dimensions, most of them having to do with their products and services. But some of them have to do—or can have to do—with the way they treat and compensate people. Other things being equal on the product side, the organization with a high-end, leading compensation system is going to be the one that will attract and retain the most interesting, the most innovative, the most energetic, the most productive employees. And by high-end I do not mean paying the most. I mean that it is like the newest, most user-friendly business hotel room, not the most costly (often at the old hotel).[2] Not so incidentally, edge-of-the-envelope compensation systems, as Norman Harberger suggested, also are structured to encourage individual laggards to leave. Hence, the organization is not lean and mean, but lean and friendly with a cadre of people who actually work during the day, all day, every day, and enjoy it.

Transformational upgrade is worrisome, but it's also exciting. We have all been through transformational changes in our adult lives—a family move, a wedding, a birth—in which we weren't sure what was going to happen. Yet despite lots of uncertainties and a lot of worry, there was still, overall, an upbeat, positive sense of the future. And there is a sense that "We can do this." That's one of the things that transformational upgrade generates. To paraphrase the old Pontiac slogan, "It builds excitement."

Finally, transformational upgrade moves at a Web-year pace. As I've remarked, a Web-year is about three months. "One step at a time" might have been an ideal way to go—once upon a time. It works much less well in a multitasking environment where simultaneity rather than series is the norm. Today, organizations need to be governed by the Boiled Frog principle: The rate of change inside your firm has to be greater than the rate of change outside your firm, or you will die.[3]

On the other hand, transformational change has some distinct disadvantages. Obviously, the bigger a change is, the harder it is, so the low-gear, hard work of transformational upgrade in the compensation system—a Rock of Gibraltar in many organizations—is potentially intimidating. There is, of course, a huge risk of failure. The bigger the upgrade goal, the more dramatic the failure seems if the upgrade is not successful.

Transformational upgrade in compensation system is particularly difficult because of the Balkanized state of current compensation systems. It might be hard even to get people to run a new system. When I talk with individuals about the possibility of becoming a compensation case manager, they often have little concept of what I'm talking about. Even after we work through the compensation equation, talking about the need to sit down with the employee and go through all the parts of the equation and allow the employee to do some customizing, they shake their heads in disbelief. Then they are likely to say, "Boy, that would be fabulous, but it will never happen. I wouldn't know what to do. I wouldn't know how to do it." And of course, that is an issue that upgrade agents have to consider.

There's another problematic piece that connects with this point. When people say, "I wouldn't know how to do it," their statement may reflect not only concern about their own skills but also a perception about the nature of organizational reality as they've come to know it. When they say, "This will never work," they are probably referring more to resistance at higher levels of the organization than to anything they don't know. For example, one of my evening MBA students had designed a work system that was based on some unusual (to the firm) compensation concepts. She worked for a software company and managed a team of about thirty-five individuals who were dedicated to a particular project. She organized the project so that the team started work Monday at lunchtime and ended Thursday more or less at close of business. The team members were able to fully complete their task for the client during that period of time. They had a roving "on-call" system so that the client was never without someone who was available to help out. Meanwhile, the individuals on the team got a quality of life bonus that money can't buy: Friday, and half of Monday. People loved it. They were highly motivated, and they worked extremely hard. It was a very successful system from every point of view, except one: my student's manager's point of view. The manager kept saying, "But people ought to be at work on Friday." When he was asked why, his answer was, "Because people have always been to work on Friday, and Monday morning, too! It's just not right if you are not here. What if something came up?" It was pointed out to him that all the work was being accomplished in this abbreviated time frame, that the customer was tremendously satisfied—and had said so orally and in writing on many occasions—and that if the system were changed, many of the team members would leave. He kept replying, "But people have to work on Friday. People have always worked on Friday." He was ready to order everyone to work on Monday and Friday, although he was told that it would in all likelihood create anger among employees and cause people to leave, resulting, overall, in decreased service to customers. (The situation had a happy, if high-maintenance, ending. He was finally convinced it could be a "pilot" project. Due to this and other rigidities, he has since moved on.)

One can see his point, or at least where he was coming from. There is no question that facetime is something his generation knew how to do expertly. Today, though, it is the enemy of sensible, accomplishment-based work organization.

For all these reasons, transformational upgrade of the compensation system requires a strategic, carefully planned design and execution that is unusual in organizational change efforts. Big upgrades require detailed planning as well as openness to new thinking, and it may be that the organizational capacity is simply not there. That doesn't mean that the change effort has to be abandoned. It may be appropriate to consider, instead, transactional change.

Transactional Upgrade

Transformational upgrade is, in a sense, deductive: it cascades down from a central strategic locus. Transactional upgrade is more of an inductive process, in the sense that it builds to the whole from the parts.

There are some advantages to transactional upgrade. For one thing, one can achieve small but beneficial upgrades and invoke either the "low-hanging fruit" or "success through small wins" approach. "Picking low-hanging fruit" means seizing opportunities for upgrades that are already in the system and putting them into the basket. The "success through small wins" approach builds on the knowledge that organizations and people get more good feeling out of small successes than the size of the win would suggest. That is one reason why I've detailed a number of specific suggestions for specific problems in preceding chapters. You don't have to move wholesale to the total compensation approach to begin leveraging relatively small improvements. The important point to keep in mind, however, is that tactical transactional change needs a strategic plan to guide the changes. It is the plan—the vision—that knits everything together and makes the various smaller parts intelligible. Otherwise tactical change looks, to the employees, like so much random activity.

Transactional upgrades can be instituted in ways to minimize the downstream possibility of big failure. Small failures can be OK; in fact, one can even create a pilot situation in which the possibility of failure is built into the initiating series of events. Pushing that approach a bit further, one can even talk about expecting certain failures in order to improve the system. So, for instance, the development of a cafeteria benefits plan is a wonderful step toward a cafeteria compensation plan. Cafeteria benefits already has some key things going for it that can lead to success, including a broad general understanding of what the approach is, and consultants with experience in assisting in implementation. It is a win-win (for employer and employee) idea that can build across-the-board interest. It embodies choice, which means that, insofar as the "medium is the message" is concerned, it is an innovation that both embodies and presages cafeteria compensation. And one can stop there, if need be. While that would not be my hope, sometimes top team support for change—any change—evaporates or goes south. In that event it is nice to have a set of transactional steps that, if the journey must stop for a while, can be useful in their own right.

This is an example of a "whole firm" change. Perhaps there are smaller "spot" pilot changes that can make a difference. A good way to start is to do an employee survey about compensation. For example, try using the Index of Difference (Chapter One) on a focus group basis to get a sense of what employees may want or need that is different from the current compensation array. Or use the Index of Difference as part of a new employee information package that gives some clues about the new hires' mind-set as opposed to the perspectives of current employees.

There are, of course, a number of disadvantages to the small upgrade approach. One is that small upgrades may, in the final analysis, not make a lot of difference because of the entrenched power of convention in the compensation system. Indeed, the accomplishments—such as they are—may prove to be only Pyrrhic victories, winning the battle but losing the war. For example, as I mentioned earlier, you may be introducing cafeteria benefits as a first step toward cafeteria compensation, and find out that the bosses are not interested in going any further. That is why each step in the transactional and tactical change process needs to be both an end and a means—an end in its own right, and a means to further, loftier ends. If you get stopped, the intermediate end (cafeteria benefits in this example) is useful in and of itself.

I want to reemphasize, however, the importance of an overall strategy. As the saying has it, "If you don't know where you're going, how will you know when you get there?" To be a successful upgrade strategy, transactional upgrade needs to be *strategically oriented* rather than simply opportunistically driven. Obviously, the "low-hanging fruit" strategy has a certain appeal. On the other hand, if the low-hanging fruits are unconnected each to the other, either conceptually or actually, so that all one is doing is taking an apple here and a prune or a plum there, the small changes may not add up to anything over time. In fact, this kind of opportunistic (or, sometimes, serendipitous) change happens frequently in organizations. It is one of the organizational developments that contribute significantly to the incoherence of the overall compensation approach. Somebody adds a benefit here, somebody else approves a perk there, with no overall rationale and no clear justification in terms of what the company expects for its investment. This is one of the most important pressures pushing compensation systems to what one employee called "confoosin systems."

In this respect, transactional upgrade and transformational upgrade actually have similar strategic requirements, even though the mode of implementation is different. Transformational change calls for a rollout strategy in which the upgrade idea has already been formulated and agreed upon. The problem here is essentially one of reorganization and implementation. In transactional change, one has an idea of what is to come, but it is more a ramp-up than a rollout strategy. Organizational upgrade agents good at one are usually good at the other too, but it's important to keep in mind that the two approaches involve different kinds of considerations. Ramp-up management requires build (sequence) control and trajectory management. Rollout management requires cascade control.

Both at Once

A variation on the transformational-versus-transactional decision is to be ready to apply either. In this case, you go in with the mind-set of a big change or upgrade, but, depending on the lay of the land, you are prepared to go either way. Here, the upgrade agent is ready for the elephant or the mouse. The advantage to this approach is that it has a certain broken-field-running appeal. That is, you go to the left and to the right, depending on what really happens with respect to support from above, buy-in from below, and so on. So, for example, you might go through a preliminary process within the HR department (involving some employees as well) to get an idea of what a reconstruction of compensation would look like and what might be involved in achieving this goal in terms of cost and time. You might also plan ways to overcome certain difficulties that you can anticipate (see the work of Herbert Simon, following in a bit). Then you move to discuss this initial thought with superiors. If you get an enthusiastic response, you might begin the transformational process; if the response is lukewarm, then perhaps smaller increments of change might be the best choice.

This "ready for either" approach avoids the potential of emotional commitment to "the one right way" that some transformational upgraders and some transactional upgraders espouse. Simultaneity also creates a kind of pincer operation where some elements of big upgrade are going down, and some elements of small upgrade are building up, thus meeting in the middle. For example, a firm can begin conceptualizing and implementing a cafeteria benefits plan as a part of a total compensation plan (big change), while beginning a focus group effort to understand employees' wishes and desires with respect to the individual-level, X-factor elements that could make worklife better (small change). This "both or one" strategy has lots of appeal, because it can take advantage of the strengths of each approach and minimize some of their disadvantages.

How Do You Choose?

Are there guidelines for picking one or the other approach to change when it comes to compensation systems? Although prediction is hazardous, there are some thoughts worth sharing. One has to do with the issue of speed and magnitude of change, as described in Table 9.1.

Table 9.1. Change Strategies as a Function of the Speed and Magnitude of Change

	Speed of Change		
Impact	Slow	Fast	Really Fast
Low			
Big		Innovate	Innovate or invent
Really big		Innovate or invent	Invent

The table conceptualizes change in terms of three speeds and three magnitudes. Since organizations handle slow and low-impact change fairly routinely, we need to pay attention only to two speeds (fast and really fast) and two magnitudes (big and really big).

Fast and big change definitely requires a certain amount of transactional change in order to prevent chaos. The type of upgrading represented by the intersection of fast and big change (innovation) is becoming the standard for organizational operation today, and there the preference may be for transactional change. The two off-diagonal cells (fast and really big, or big and really fast) suggest the "both at once" strategy, being ready to jump whichever way the wind might be blowing in a fast-changing environment. Finally, in a situation of really big, really fast change, transformational efforts are absolutely required. Transactional efforts will not work when an organization runs into change of large magnitude and great speed. That's a time for total reinvention. A problem, however, is that if you get to a point where you must have transformation, it is all the more likely that that transformation will be accomplished by someone else, and part of the transformation has the top team looking for other jobs!

The bottom line is that much of the decision about whether to use transformational or transactional approaches depends on the velocity and churning of the environment. If one is in turbulent white water, one is going to need an appropriate craft. A canoe won't do it. You've got to move to a rubber raft. Plaintive cries that "My compensation system has always been a canoe" simply are unacceptable.

Within this broad framework, however, some other variables might be worth considering. For example, take yourself. As a compensation change agent, are you more comfortable with striving for big change all at once, or are you more of a "one step at a time" kind of person? Taking into account your own skills and preferences may suggest a way to go. If somebody wants music at a wedding, and you play the violin, it would be best if that's what you played. If the group says, "We were hoping for a trumpet," say, "Well, I can play the violin for you. If you want a trumpet, you'd better get the other guy." Being forced or seduced into using techniques in which you are not proficient adds to the risk of failure by a substantial factor.

Another consideration has to do with your ability in what Rosabeth Moss Kanter calls "coalition building."[4] She outlines a series of steps that have enduring value for any kind of change. While she does not apply these steps to compensation change specifically, they work wonderfully.

1. *Clearing the investment:* This step involves checking with the immediate superior about the compensation change plan, getting strategic and tactical suggestions, getting the green light, and keeping the superior informed about the progress of the compensation change.
2. *Preselling and making cheerleaders:* For this step, first go lower, then higher in the organization. Preselling involves securing support from those below you, and convincing them of the potentials and possibilities of compensation change. Making cheerleaders involves identifying those—sometimes called opinion leaders—who can and will both speak in favor of the project and influence others positively.

3. *Horse trading:* This is a classic element in change efforts. It involves, as Kanter says, "offering promises of payoffs from the project in exchange for support."[5]
4. *Securing blessings:* Finally, with the initial steps complete, you can go to the top brass—the "organizational archbishops"—for an *imprimatur,* or blessing. Top brass like to know that there is some considerable support for change, but at the same time they don't want to feel sandbagged or as if they have been handed a fait accompli to rubber-stamp. How much support from the top do you have? Is it lasting support? As pressure and resistance begin to develop, will that support evaporate? If your judgment is that senior management will bail when the rubber hits the road, then perhaps it's better to consider transactional upgrades. You'll have enough problems without finding that top management isn't walking the talk.

Maintaining this balance—a dance of change—in which you manage slightly up, then down, then across, then way up is often the difference between successful change and a failed effort.

■ The Problems

Regardless of the type of upgrade approach you adopt, you will run into a fairly standard set of problems. Nobel Prize–winning economist Herbert Simon, from Carnegie Mellon University, identified them some years ago.[6] Simon was looking at the general case of problems in organizational upgrade and identified five typical problems that will always need to be dealt with. He called them the "costs of change"; I call them the "costs of upgrade." They are as follows: inertia, self-interest, rationality, subordination, and cultural lag. I have added a sixth cost to the list: structural lag.

1. Inertia

The inertia problem simply means that it is difficult to get individuals to do things differently from the way they have done them before. This is the low-gear problem of upgrade. Even when individuals recognize that they need to upgrade, they sometimes lack the energy to take the steps to make the situation better. This is true even when the technology is available and the effort is minimal. Obviously when the technology is uncertain and the required effort is greater, the resistance due to inertia builds. People are likely to prefer complaining to changing. Compensation change is among the more difficult to achieve because of the multiplicity of values attached to it.

2. Self-Interest

While inertia plays a role in upgrade resistance, one cannot ignore the possibility that simple self-interest is at work. Apart from the energy that might be required to overcome organizational inertia, individual workers will have to expend a bit more energy, and that may entail some costs. For example, if my employer introduces a new software program for writing documents, I may be reluctant to switch from my currently preferred program, even if it isn't as good. That's the inertia problem. But there may also be some self-interest costs associated with the switch. For example, initially I'm going to make some mistakes and will be less efficient. For another example, there are organizational and self-interest costs in switching from a deferred benefit retirement plan (in which the employee, with some combination of age and years in rank, is guaranteed a proportion of last year's salary) to a defined contribution plan (in which the employer puts a certain amount of money into a retirement vehicle, usually along with the employee). The organizational costs involve switching over from one to another. The personal employee costs involve the fact that employees now have to pay attention to the investment elements and make decisions about how their retirement dollars are going to be invested.

3. Rationality

One of the elements that differentiate humans from dogs is that we like explanations of why things are, or need to be the way they are. I do explain a lot of things to my own dog, but it does not seem to matter. When I became a parent, I vowed that one thing that I would never say was "Because I said so." I think I was a parent for maybe eight or nine seconds when I began to use that phrase, and of course I've used it consistently throughout my parenthood. As tough as it may be to break the habit, the problem with the "Because I said so" explanation is that it substitutes authority for thought. In the context of organizational change, explanations are usually available, but they have to be formulated and delivered to employees. If firms are going to upgrade their compensation plans, they must appropriately and candidly discuss some of the problems with the current plan and explain in a straightforward way how the new approach will not only address these issues but also add value over and above rectifying historical problems.

But rationality problems have another wrinkle, beyond the need for explanation. Especially for new information, lots of repeating—I said lots of repeating—is needed because of selective perception. Typically, what is required is *over*communication. I can't tell you how many times I have sat in front of a classroom and said to my MBA students, "The exam is Thursday, December 15th, at 2 P.M., in this room. Are there any questions?" Immediately one or two hands go up. I call on Sid, who seems to be in every class. "Yes, Sid?" "Uh, professor, when is the exam and where will it be?" No matter how clear you think you are being, say it again. And again.

4. Subordination

Simon calls his fourth problem the subordination problem. By "subordination," he refers to the twin issues of being uninvolved in matters that affect you and being told what to do or being the subject of power. I have mentioned employee involvement so often that I am sure it is becoming tiresome. Nonetheless, people do need to be involved in designing the plans that affect them. This is perhaps especially true in the compensation arena because of the many-leveled importance of compensation. Yet, perhaps because of its high importance, this is one area where employers are relatively less likely to ask employees what they think and want. Companies often survey their employees on far less weighty issues, but they treat compensation as the exclusive province of the people who own and manage the business. If employees are not involved, then they have no buy-in for the plan and hence no reason to pay attention to it and help make it work. Further, resentment over high-handedness may create the very real possibility of opposition and even sabotage. And finally, absent employee build-in, employers lose the chance to connect with employees, not only about the components of the plan, but at the emotional level. Over and above any particular benefits of employee involvement, the outreach effort conveys the larger, and useful, message that employees matter and that employers care about them.

5. Cultural Lag

Sometimes the kind of upgrade that is needed conflicts with "the way we have always done things around here," or "our culture," or "the company way." In the case of compensation, you may hear, "We've always paid market," or "We've always paid below market," or "We've always paid above market." Such truisms become truths engraved as commandments in the company tablets. As practices become sacred practices, they become even more difficult to upgrade. Cultural lag is a sociological term for a situation that occurs when a structure—the market, the local or national employment scene, whatever—changes faster than the values connected with prior situations do. Culture then lags behind structure.

The culture problem often is made even more difficult by a lack of recognition that it is a problem. Let me give a typical family example. Suppose that your oldest son grows up, gets married, and moves out of town. This new situation is a change in family structure. He and his new wife want to come back for Thanksgiving weekend. However, her parents also live in the area, and each set of parents wants the young couple to show up for Thanksgiving dinner on Thanksgiving Day. "It just wouldn't be Thanksgiving if we didn't have you here," each family says. Now, a lot of possibilities for harmony exist here—a joint dinner, or for one of the families to have Thanksgiving dinner on Friday, Saturday, or Sunday. However, many people feel, "Well, that's just not the way we have done things." Thanksgiving has become a sacred ritual; structural change dictates a change in the ritual, but emotionally, it is difficult. That's where the lack of problem recognition comes in. Thanksgiving is a day like other days, and there is no reason that one can't entertain some flexibility about it. When people don't even recognize that flexibility might be an option, they are experiencing what I have called *culture lock.* That is, their value system locks them into the one best way and creates a number of difficult situations with respect to upgrade.

Because of the value-laden elements attached to the compensation system, it becomes difficult to contemplate certain important elements. For example, if you reward people, in part at least, according to the accomplishments they produce, then if they produce no accomplishments they should get no bonus or increase. But even hardened managers have trouble with the "zero increase" policy. Or consider turnover. We have the idea that high turnover is inherently bad. *It's not!* High turnover among the people in the lowest 20 percent of producers (remember Harberger's principles) is good. If you have very little turnover, you are probably retaining exactly those people you wish would move on. But it is hard to get these culturally magical ideas out of our heads.

By the same token, an employee may say, "I am *entitled* to full medical benefits. Anything less is wrong." Or an employer may say, "It's not good business to allow people to customize their compensation." Exactly what the basis of these ideas might be, no one can say. True, those who are resistant to change might have tradition on their side. But business ideas are always being upgraded as conditions change. Why not compensation?

6. Structural Lag

Structural lag is the opposite of cultural lag. In the former, situations change while ideas lag behind. In the latter, new values are in place but organizational practices lag behind. Thus, the new values of Gen X employees are often frustrated by the practices of older managers and organizations. Flextime and job sharing, for example, are highly prized by newer young families, yet they are often prohibited by more traditional policies.

■ Suggested Solutions

Never just a theorist, Herbert Simon provided some suggested solutions or antidotes for the problems of upgrade he identified. Let me summarize and build on some of his ideas here.

1. Inertia

The inertia problem is the get-off-the-dime-and-start problem. Simon makes two suggestions: make compliance easy, and make noncompliance difficult.

Simon uses the example of federal income-tax withholding. Compliance is easy, since the company does the withholding. Noncompliance is difficult, since there's no alternative. Another example is bottle-return laws. In Michigan, for instance, consumers pay ten cents for every bottle or can. The checkout person won't hand over the beer without collecting the dime, so there's little choice but to pay up. Compliance is easy; noncompliance is impossible. We may grumble, we may grouse, we may swear and cuss. We still pay the dime and take the beer.

In thinking about any kind of upgrade in the compensation system, therefore, we need to think along two dimensions: how to make it easy to do the new thing, and how to make it difficult or impossible to do the old thing. The built-in reinforcement structure will move people more quickly from old to new. Whatever upgrade in the compensation system is selected, it is important to set it up so that employees have strong incentives to move to the new—and no incentives to remain with the old. For example, in moving to a flexible benefit system, setting a specific date for the changeover rather than a period of time for it makes compliance easy. You gotta do it. Noncompliance is impossible—if you do not study the new forms and make your choices, Human Resources does the conversion for you.

Nike has captured the essence of the solution to inertia in its motto, "Just do it!"

2. Self-Interest

The self-interest problem concerns the personal costs and disruptions that accompany any upgrade. When I take a job in another city, for example, there are going to be a host of disturbances involved: selling my house, moving, seeking new schools for my kids, seeking to identify appropriate employment for my wife, and so on. None of this means, necessarily, that I won't take an exciting new job, but the disturbances can be daunting.

Simon suggests *recognizing* and *managing* the inevitable disturbances. For example, if the company assigns me a moving coordinator who begins to handle all of the thousand and one details that I am worried about, that will prevent a build-up of negative orientation based on self-interest problems. If on top of that the company is relatively appropriate in providing compensation and doesn't try to nickel-and-dime me, my attitude is going to be much more positive. My job upgrade has costs associated with it, and addressing them is important.

More broadly, cafeteria compensation is a direct response to self-interest issues. Individuals in such a system need to pay attention to what they actually want, and that involves a cost in energy and even new skills. Hence the compensation case manager. Over time the need to consult with the case manager will trail off, but initially providing time and expertise to the employees will pay big dividends. To take another example, as part of the move to a defined contribution mode for retirement, the company might hire consultants to assist employees in thinking through their assignments and distributions among bonds, stocks, money market funds, and real estate. As time passes, employees can do more of this themselves, but at the start some assistance would be helpful.

3. Rationality

The antidote to the "Because I said so" way of presenting a new approach is to think through why we're doing what we're doing, develop a set of appropriate rationales, and articulate those rationales. This is basically what Simon suggests. He argues that employers need to develop justifications for an organizational change and communicate those reasons.

Developing justifications is actually a boon for both the firm and the employees. Perhaps there is no area in the firm where explanations are needed more than in compensation. If employees are to understand what they are being paid for, then explanation is required. If employees are to understand what the goals are toward which they need to work, then explanation is required. If employees are to understand how the incentive system actually works (and why), then explanation is required. There is a fabulous benefit to employers here. You actually have to think through what you are doing in order to explain it. The painful process of asking yourself why you are paying people is a necessary precursor to explaining it to them. Clarifying it to yourself, and for yourself, is a vital first step.

But developing justifications is not enough. They need to be shared, over and over again. This may seem like a bit of a no-brainer. Why would you develop justifications if you didn't communicate them? But we all are aware of many situations in which "Corporate" has a lot of reasons why things ought to happen, but somehow fails to share them. They know what's going on; everyone else is in the dark. Communication also needs to be in several media. In any employee group, even small ones, there are differences in how individual employees learn and absorb information. Some like to read it; others like to see it on video or in a personal presentation; others like to hear it on audiotape or in person. Different modes appeal to different people. And, for any one person, the "two-media rule" often applies. This principle suggests that if I receive a communication through two media, I am more than twice as likely to absorb it because of the mutually reinforcing spiral of the two modes through which information is being conveyed.

4. Subordination

American society is participation-oriented. Earlier I mentioned the Boston Tea Party as an example of this principle at work in our history. Employees share this cultural value. Hence, in any upgrade effort, whether transactional or transformational, it's important to involve those affected. Employees might not go so far as to say, "No compensation without representation," but you get the idea. Without build-in, you're not going to get buy-in. It is as simple—or as complex—as that.

There are a variety of mechanisms through which employee input can be garnered. Employees can be involved through focus groups, participatory committees, surveys, and other means so that their views can be ascertained, sifted, and sorted—and so that they know they are being listened to.

The complex part comes from the fact that while employers often like to ask employees what they think, they don't always like to follow what employees suggest they do. That's always been a puzzle to me. Although you cannot follow every suggestion—they are sometimes contradictory—many times the things employees suggest are easy to do; they're simple things, and employers could get lots of points simply by doing them. But they don't. I was in a firm not long ago that had a shredder mounted outside of a suite of cubicles. Someone had tacked a sign above the shredder that said "Suggestion Box." Need I say more?

A good principle to remember is that "the price of feedback is feedback." If you ask employees what they think, then feed back (rationality principle here) what the gist of their response was, and what you are able to do and why. (And of course, what you cannot do and why not.)

5. Cultural Lag

Trying to get organizations to upgrade sacred values is going to be problematic, and this is especially true when money in all of

its symbolic aspects becomes involved. Simon makes two suggestions, and I will add a third.

The first idea he shares is to identify the plan with valued
symbols. In other words, take advantage of the fact that cultures
conflict. So, for example, if a company is tied to the idea of
"equality in pay" (I'm not referring here to equal pay for equal
work, but rather to equality as in "across the board increases"),
then one can invoke a competing value, "achievement," and in-
dicate how a more differentially oriented pay system responds
well to that American value. In the benefits area, where people
believe that they should be "sponsored" for entitlement programs (say, sick days), one can introduce a competing value of
"earning" and its values. That might mean that employees earn
some cash back if they do not take their sick days. Rarely does
one lack for a competing value that can be brought into play. Uncover and use them.

Simon's second suggestion is to adjust the plan to prevail-
ing symbols. This means to seek to connect the upgrade efforts
to other symbols that the organization cherishes. For example,
if the organization considers itself a leader in its field, then being
a leader in the compensation field would have some appeal. If
the organization considers itself innovative and edge-of-the-
envelope, then innovative and edge-of-the-envelope compensation systems would have some appeal.

One can attach new plans to people as well as ideas. This
is where support from the top team comes in. If, for example,
the CEO, the CFO, and others convincingly articulate the need
for upgrade in the direction that we are discussing, that's going to give your efforts a major boost. If, on the other hand, the
CFO waffles and is unclear or evasive, you're pretty much dead
meat.

To these suggestions, I would add, "Don't trash the past."
There's a tremendous pressure when introducing either transformational or transactional upgrades to talk about "the bad old
days" and the great news that they are going to be replaced by

the good new days. The difficulty is that everybody you need to implement the good new days contributed to the bad old days. Hence, even if the old days were bad, there's no point in forcing people to admit it. What that does is create a self-protective layer of denial that drains energy and takes emphasis and focus away from the upgrade effort. Instead, say the good old days are now going to be replaced by the even better new days. Help people feel that the upgrade builds on the past rather than destroying the past.

Cultural lag involves values change, one of the very difficult kinds of change. It is more involved in compensation change because of the many values that money has. Compensation change agents may need to employ several ongoing techniques. Exposing top leadership and shop floor employees to new ideas on a fairly regular basis is one approach. Obviously, not all new ideas will be ones that the change agent wants to promote; in fact, some of them may be really weird. However, seeing what others are thinking and doing can help leaders and employees to rethink their own positions. And the really weird ideas have their purposes as well. Once people stop laughing at them, the changes you are proposing—dramatic, yes, but not as weird—look much more acceptable.

6. Structural Lag

Structural lag occurs when new wine is trapped in old bottles, where new compensation wishes cannot be implemented because of old compensation structures. Here consultants can be very useful. They can survey the employees, provide top management with some of the wishes and desires of the "new" employees, and begin a process of updating. Of course, consultants are not always necessary. A company can begin this process on its own, using employees who are thought of as opinion leaders and statespersons to take a broader view and begin the process internally.

■ Concluding Suggestions

I've so far discussed the general problems that can be anticipated in any organizational upgrade, and some solutions to
them. Let me conclude with a few tips on how to get going with
an upgrade effort in the compensation area.

First, a customized rewards program needs to be custom-
designed. You need to walk the talk. There are no off-the-shelf
solutions. There are, however, places to get some ideas. Worldat-
Work, previously the American Compensation Association,
maintains a Total Rewards Newsletter. (The association's Web
address is http://www.worldatwork.org. The newsletter address is totalrewards@listsrv.worldatwork.org.) That's a great
place for ideas, for finding out what's hot and what's not, and
for getting some additional thoughts going.

Second, as with all upgrade efforts, you need to start where
the organization is. What the organization needs and what it can
tolerate may be two different things. Indeed, it may be the case
that the organization needs transformational upgrade and will
not tolerate it and will therefore die. My advice in that case is to
move on. The old saw, "You can lead a horse to water, but you
can't make it drink," applies here, as does the saying, "Never
argue with a drunk." Sometimes an organization is drunk on
history, tradition, its own way, and so forth, and because of that
inebriated state it is unable to process the information that the
upgrade agent is bringing. In fact, in many cases, what happens
to the upgrade agent as the messenger of the new way is that the
messenger is killed—or at least fired.

Assuming your organization is at least somewhat open to
change, a good place to start is to use the KSS methodology. KSS
stands for Keep, Stop, and Start. It is a simple, low-impact, and
nontechnical method for information seeking, and it also paves
the way for change. *Keep* means "What are we doing in compensation that's good and that we ought to keep on doing?" *Stop*

means "Are there things in compensation that are not good, which we ought to phase out?" And probably most important, *Start* means "Are there things in compensation that we are not now doing and that we should initiate?" To implement KSS, one prepares a form that asks employees' perspectives about the current compensation system along these dimensions and then uses the feedback as a basis for initiating changes (see Exhibit 9.1 for an example). Typically compensation change agents feed back the results to those who filled it out (remember—the price of feedback is feedback!).

The data you collect will provide a wealth of information that will allow you to begin an upgrade process in a way that is connected with the kinds of upgrades that many of those affected would very much like to see. One caveat about using KSS, though: Don't start it if you're not committed to going through with it.

And there is a danger that employees will be asking for lots of things you cannot provide. One expert who reviewed this chapter made the following comment:

> I'm also concerned that people will not find it realistic to give employees such an open-ended questionnaire about compensation (and the promise of a system that changes every year) without a *lot* of groundwork being laid (if then). I'm sure my last company, a pretty enlightened place, would not have gone near this as it's presented, on the grounds that people would ask for all kinds of wild and unfeasible things, putting the company on the defensive as it tries to explain why they can't be done. If it were up to me, I'd leave out the figure and let people work out for themselves how they might use KSS.

The guy has a point. However, I thought I would leave the suggestion and put in his caution. (He is a pretty cautious guy anyway.) Obviously one cannot provide everything for everyone. On the other hand, as I have suggested throughout, there

Exhibit 9.1. A Sample KSS Form for Compensation

Transcendental Technologies Compensation Feedback Form

Transcendental Technologies is interested in what you think about the way you are compensated. Your compensation includes base pay, bonuses, and benefits. You may be satisfied with those now, or you might like some different kind of mix among them, assuming the total dollar amount remains the same. Then, too, there may be other things you would like as compensation from your workplace, such as an account to help you buy some supplies and equipment you need, learning opportunities, more time, or something unique only to you. While we are not promising anything, we would like to know what you think because that helps us plan, with you, for a new and improved compensation system for next year.

Below are three areas labeled Keep, Stop, and Start. Under Keep, please tell us what you think is good about our current plan that should be retained. Under Stop, please share with us those things that are out of date or no longer needed and should be stopped or phased out. Under Start, please let us know things that we are not now doing that you would like to see us consider.

It is our view that "the price of feedback is feedback." In next month's e-zine we will present a summary of what the overall suggestions have been for further reflection and refinement. Thank you.

Keep: What should we *keep*?

Stop: What is not working that we should *stop or phase out*?

Start: What do we not now have that we should initiate or *start*?

---

might be much more firms could provide if they knew about it. Consider pet health care, for example. Requests for something like this are increasing, a trend echoed by my MBA students who work in human resources. When I first mentioned this idea to some of my HR colleagues a number of years ago—partially in jest—I was greeted with derision. One of the listeners said "Sure John, pet-i-care. Just what a professor would come up with! Next thing it will be plumb-i-care! [He meant insurance for plumbing problems.] You guys are just too much!" Well, too much or not, its day has arrived. And while we do not have plumb-i-care at the university yet my energy company (DTE Energy in Detroit—the electric and gas company) offers a prepaid package that will take care of all my furnace and electric appliance needs for a monthly fee. As yet, my employer is not picking this up, but, guess what, I have just suggested it!

My reviewer's point is a serious one, however. Requests for feedback and opinion must be handled with great care. Do not ask for what you do not want to hear. Manage the expectations at the front end. Consider using a focus group for small-scale information excursions. And if this approach to KSS does not appeal, configure it as you like.

Finally, you might consider the six steps that WorldatWork suggests:[7]

1. Identify the unique external and internal influences for your organization.
2. Inventory all the possible elements of compensation, benefits, and the work experience and weigh the importance of each relative to the influences identified above.
3. Assess the total rewards mix of your current organization both in terms of dollars and people dedicated to these [that is, assigned to work on the rewards mix] today.
4. Listen to your employees and employment candidates regarding the relative importance of various reward elements.

5. Map the interrelationships of the components as you consider individual programs in each area and the total rewards "package" that will be the unique competitive advantage for your organization. Ask, what is your aspirational strategy (where do you hope to go) compared to where you are today?

6. Create the mix of the components that most effectively ensures the behaviors and culture you need to achieve your ultimate business strategy.

CHAPTER SUMMARY

Upgrading a compensation system is very difficult in part because of the combination of practical and symbolic value that money represents. Yet upgrading is essential to compete effectively in the world of today, and more so in the world of tomorrow.

Upgrade strategies may be transformational or transactional. Each approach has its advantages and disadvantages. It's also possible to use a combination of strategies. But regardless of what strategy is chosen, a vision of what the ultimate change would look like is essential. The vision presented in this book is one of an employee-driven rewards system that brings all the elements of compensation together and allows for a substantial degree of customization and choice.

Regardless of which upgrade path is chosen, there are costs associated with any change, no matter how positive: inertia costs, cultural costs, self-interest costs, rationality costs, subordination costs, and structural lag costs. These costs must be anticipated, addressed, and managed. If they are, and if the solutions are customized to the firm's unique environment, then the likelihood of success is high.

Appendix: A Look at Compensation Issues in the Public and Nonprofit Sectors

The kinds of problems that I described in Chapter One regarding old pay in the business sector, and that Don Lowman stresses, are also present in two other important sectors—the public sector and the nonprofit or independent sector.

The public sector is a substantial employer, with equally pressing needs for efficiency and effectiveness. With respect to governmental organizations, Howard Risher asks, "Are public employers ready for a 'new pay' program?"[1] By way of responding to his own question, he outlines eleven problems with old pay. According to Risher, the traditional (public sector) compensation model

- Reinforces the importance of the job hierarchy at a time when organizations are trying to downplay their hierarchical differences to promote teamwork

Note: Professor Michael D. Johnson of the University of Michigan Business School prepared this case study. The case is intended as a learning exercise rather than to illustrate either effective or ineffective handling of a situation. The company names and the data in the case have been changed to preserve confidentiality.

- Overemphasizes salary grade changes and promotions as the basis for salary increases rather than focusing on the need to develop and enhance job competence
- Inspires "game playing" and dishonesty as the basis for justifying a higher salary grade
- Hinders organizational change and downsizing, since all job changes have to be reevaluated under traditional compensation programs
- Perpetuates overly rigid and inflexible rules governing compensation
- Creates a sense of entitlement if pay is increased across the board
- Takes too much time and costs too much to maintain
- Requires excessive time to prepare for and make administrative decisions
- Perpetuates bureaucratic management
- Establishes implicit limits on what employees are willing to do, since their pay is based on the duties listed in their job descriptions
- Creates tension between line managers and human resources staff who are required to defend the program's principles and police the decision process

His answer, then, is that the sector needs a more contemporary approach, but, as with the private sector, change will be hard.

The story is much the same when it comes to nonprofit organizations. The *NonProfit Times*'s Paul Clolery reports that times are tight and competition is stiff, even in a downshifted compensation arena:

The sky didn't fall for the Year 2000 and neither did nonprofit salaries, according to a new study of readers of *The NonProfit Times*. A booming economy in most of the nation has workers in short supply. The market is tight even in areas that are not doing as well economically.

A survey form was sent to a cross section of *NPT* readers for this 12th annual study of paychecks. The results are based on nearly 300 responses. The responses showed boards scrambling to make organizational efficiencies to pay for salaries.

Chief executives will earn a projected 3 percent more in fiscal 2000 and chief financial officers' pay will remain flat at roughly $56,033.

Program officers can also expect a 3 percent raise to $54,311 and volunteer directors a scant 1 percent, averaging $36,042.[2]

The overall picture of the compensation structure, however, while downshifted as I mentioned, is much the same as the points made by Lowman and Risher. It is traditional, with a heavy emphasis on salary and raises. It is quintessential old pay. If anything, the governmental and nonprofit worlds will have a more difficult time than the corporate sector will moving to upgraded, accomplishment-based compensation systems because "accomplishments" are harder to identify.

Notes

Preface

1. Lance Armstrong with Sally Jenkins, *It's Not About the Bike: My Journey Back to Life* (New York: Putnam, 2000).
2. William C. Byham with Jeff Cox, *Zapp! The Lightning of Empowerment: How to Improve Productivity, Quality, and Employee Satisfaction,* rev. ed. (New York: Ballantine, 1998).

Chapter One

1. Edward E. Lawler III, *Pay and Organizational Development* (Reading, Mass.: Addison Wesley, 1983).
2. W. Edwards Deming, *Out of the Crisis* (Cambridge, Mass.: MIT/CAES, 1982).
3. Edward E. Lawler III, *Strategic Pay: Aligning Organizational Strategies and Pay Systems* (San Francisco: Jossey-Bass, 1990).
4. Jay Schuster and Patricia Zingheim, *New Pay: Linking Employee and Organizational Performance* (San Francisco: Jossey-Bass, 1992).
5. Edward E. Lawler III, *Rewarding Excellence* (San Francisco: Jossey-Bass, 2000).
6. Patricia Zingheim and Jay Schuster, *Pay Them Right!* (San Francisco: Jossey-Bass, 2000).

□

7. Jerry McAdams, *The Reward Plan Advantage* (San Francisco: Jossey-Bass, 1996).
8. McAdams, *The Reward Plan Advantage,* p. 5.
9. Steve Kerr, "An Academy Classic: On the Folly of Rewarding A While Hoping for B," *Academy of Management Executive* 9, no. 1 (1995): 7–14. (Originally published in 1975!)
10. Robert Merton, *Social Structure and Process,* rev. ed. (Itasca, N.Y.: Free Press, 1957).
11. Douglas McGregor, *The Human Side of Enterprise* (New York: McGraw-Hill, 1960).
12. Scott Adams, *The Dilbert Principle* (New York: HarperCollins, 1996).
13. Thomas C. Schelling, "Egonomics, or the Art of Self-Management," *American Economic Review: Papers and Proceedings* 68, no. 2 (May 1978): 290–294.
14. Richard Thaler and Howard M. Shiffrin, "An Economic Theory of Self-Control," *Journal of Political Economy* 89, no. 21 (1981): 392–404.
15. Gareth Morgan, *Images of Organization* (Thousand Oaks, Calif.: Sage, 1986), p. 43, Exhibit 3.1.
16. Stan Davis and Jay Botkin, *The Monster Under the Bed* (New York: Simon and Schuster, 1994).
17. Daniel Yankelovich, *New Rules* (New York: Random House, 1981).
18. Sloan Wilson, *The Man in the Grey Flannel Suit* (New York: Simon and Schuster, 1955).
19. Vivian Ying Yao, my graduate student, provided the information for Table 1.3 in a personal communication; see also Claire Rains, *Beyond Generation X* (Menlo Park, Calif.: Crisp, 1998).
20. Ellen Galinsky, James T. Bond, and Dana E. Friedman, *National Study of the Changing Workforce* (New York: Families and Work Institute, 1993), p. 86.
21. Schuster and Zingheim, *New Pay.*
22. Schuster and Zingheim, *New Pay,* p xi.
23. Peter Capelli, "A Market-Driven Approach to Retaining Talent," *Harvard Business Review* (January/February, 2000): 103–111.
24. *Wall Street Journal* (January 1, 2000): B1.
25. Capelli, "A Market-Driven Approach," p. 107.

Chapter Two

1. From a pamphlet called *Total Rewards* that announced the change of name from the American Compensation Association to WorldatWork, and the enlarged focus of the new organization. Spring 2000, pp. 4–5.
2. John Naisbett, *Megatrends* (New York: Warner, 1982).
3. One way to calculate investment compensation is to cost out the package that one would use to recruit an employee, which usually includes base pay, benefits, agreed-upon supplies, perks, and so on. However, employers often do not add the cost of recruiting itself to this investment cost, so the total cost picture is usually even worse than employers think. Because money for salaries and wages and recruiting is located in two different budget lines, costs are sometimes hidden.
4. Terry Satterfield, "A Step-by-Step Approach to Developing an Effective Pay Philosophy." *American Compensation Association News* (September 1999): 22–27.

Chapter Three

1. Thomas J. Stanley and William D. Danko, *The Millionaire Next Door* (New York: Pocket Books, 1996).
2. Thorstein Veblen, *Theory of the Leisure Class* (New York: Kelly, 1965). (First published in 1899.)
3. *US News and World Report,* 127, no. 19 (November 19, 1999): 18.
4. According to the *ACA News* (January 2000), p. 15, knowledge gets the biggest premium. See also http://www.bls.gov, the Bureau of Labor Statistics site, which has lots of income information on it.

Chapter Four

1. Edward Lawler III, "Rev Up Old-Line Firms by Slimming Down CEO Perks," *USA Today* (April 27, 2000): 17A.
2. W. Edwards Deming, *Out of Crisis* (Cambridge, Mass.: Center for Advanced Engineering Study, MIT, 1986).
3. Jill Rosenfeld, "These Lawyers are Red Hot," *Fast Company* 34 (May 2000): 74.

4. Robert Frank and Phillip Cook, *The Winner-Take-All Society: Why the Few at the Top Get So Much More Than the Rest of Us* (New York: Penguin Books, 1995).
5. Stephanie Armour, "Learning Life's Not Fair in a Tight Labor Market," *USA Today* (August 16, 2000): 2A.
6. Armour, "Learning Life's Not Fair," 2B.
7. Readers may want to refer to information at http://www.gainsharing.com. The stricter definition of the term involves some differences such as the following between gainsharing and profit sharing: profit sharing is usually annual, gainsharing monthly; profit sharing does not have line of sight; profit sharing does not have the strict measures of performance. Hence I am including gainsharing under incentive pay.
8. Armour, "Learning Life's Not Fair," 2B.
9. Edward Lawler III, *Strategic Pay* (San Francisco: Jossey-Bass, 1990), p. 7.
10. Lawler, *Strategic Pay,* p. 12.
11. Some might think that long-term incentives are just for executives. Although they are popular with that group, the idea is moving out. As I suggest, long term can relate either to longer measures of *gain,* or contribution, or refer to the way in which the incentive is paid.
12. Typically, long-term incentives are used in executive compensation, and extend over longer terms than these—and may even be tied to later performance of the organization in the marketplace.
13. Donald Hastings, "Lincoln Electric's Harsh Lessons from International Expansion," *Harvard Business Review* 77, no. 3 (May/June, 1999): 162ff.
14. Steve Kerr, "An Academy Classic: On the Folly of Rewarding A While Hoping for B," *Academy of Management Executive* 9, no. 1 (1995): 7–14. (Originally published in 1975.)
15. Folly, of course, has a long history that goes far beyond the issue of incentive pay. In her book *The March of Folly,* historian Barbara Tuchman talks about folly as a really rotten decision. But her "folly" has some properties that expand Kerr's thinking. For Tuchman, folly has to be a really bad decision that is made organizationally, not by one deranged person, and one in which other choices, which were available at the time, have been rejected.

16. Deming's famous exercise, "The Red Beads" illustrates this issue elegantly. See Deming, *Out of Crisis,* pp. 110–112.
17. Gordon Fairclough, "Listen Up, Managers: Fat Paychecks Don't Always Guarantee Success," *Wall Street Journal* (March 23, 1999): B1.
18. Alfi Kohn, *Punished by Rewards: The Trouble with Gold Stars, Incentive Plans, A's, Praise, and Other Bribes* (Boston: Houghton Mifflin, 1993).
19. There is much talk about separating appraisal decisions from pay decisions. I think the reason for this line of thinking is that managers find themselves required to give appraisals for which they are untrained around measures they do not have. In that case separation is probably a good idea. In the well-run case, however, a connection makes the whole thing real. That gets everyone's attention.
20. I want to thank Jerry McAdams for making this connection explicit.
21. Frank and Cook, *The Winner-Take-All Society.*
22. Edward Lawler III, *Pay and Organizational Development* (Reading, Mass.: Addison Wesley, 1981), p. 27.
23. Monica Langly, "The House, the Money—It'll All Be Yours; There's Just One Thing," *Wall Street Journal* (November 17, 1999): A1.
24. Lawler, *Pay and Organization Development,* p. 24
25. Lawler, "Rev Up Old-Line Firms," p. 17A.
26. Paul Gilles, "Getting More Bang for Your Buck," *ACA News* (January 2000): 41–43.

Chapter Five

1. For a detailed discussion of benefits, see Richard I. Henderson, *Compensation Management in a Knowledge-Based World,* 8th ed. (Upper Saddle River, N.J.: Prentice Hall, 2000), Chapter 17. A good source of information is the Employee Benefits Research Institute (http://www.ebri.org). Another is Benefits Link (http://www.benefitslink.com/index.shtml).
2. Companies differ a great deal in terms of what they put into the benefit package, and how much employees contribute (in medical plans, for example) for it. The trend is to seek to limit employer contributions (through cafeteria benefits) and increase employee choice and contribution.

3. See Susan Lambert, "Workplace Policies as Social Policy," *Social Service Review* 67, no. 2 (June 1993): 238–260.

4. Some of this money (the employee's FICA portion and any medical insurance and retirement contribution) do come from the employee, so the employer's cost may be a bit reduced below the total percentage.

5. Patricia Zingheim and Jay Schuster, *Pay People Right* (San Francisco: Jossey-Bass, 2000), p. 43.

6. Joel Lapointe and Jo Ann Verdine, "How to Calculate the Cost of Human Resources," *Personnel Journal* (January 1988): 34–45.

7. See Jay Schuster and Patricia Zingheim, *The New Pay* (New York: Lexington Books, 1992), chapter 16, for a good discussion of flexible benefits.

8. There are lots of sources on the Net for cafeteria benefits. One—The Employee Benefit Institute of America—is a good place to start: http://www.ebia.com/.

9. Carol Gentry, "Doctor Yes: How is Merrill Lynch Limiting Health Costs? By Expanding Benefits," *Wall Street Journal* (May 23, 2000): B1.

10. Richard A. White, "Employee Preferences for Nontaxable Compensation Offered in a Cafeteria Compensation Plan: An Empirical Study, *Accounting Review* 57, no. 3 (July 1983): 539–561.

Chapter Six

1. However, some job-related equipment—supplies and the like—is portable, whether or not the employer meant it to travel with a departing employee.

2. Richard Henderson, *Compensation Management,* 7th ed. (Upper Saddle River, N.J.: Prentice Hall, 1997), p. 529.

3. Richard Henderson, *Compensation Management,* 8th ed. (Upper Saddle River, N.J.: Prentice Hall, 2000), p. 22.

4. The list is from the Wired Web site: http://www.wired.com/news/topstories/0,1287,20972,00.html. Accessed October 11, 2000.

5. Patrick McGeehan, "Merrill Joins Wall Street Rush to Keep Employees Happy," *New York Times* (May 12, 2000): C2.

6. Tom Brown, "A Passion for Perks," *Industry Week* 239, no. 7 (April 2, 1990): 64.

7. Rex Toh, C. Pat Fleenor, and David Arnesen, "Frequent Flyer Games: The Problem of Employee Abuse," *Academy of Management Executive* 7, no. 1 (February 1993): 60–72.

Chapter Seven

1. Stan Davis and Jim Botkin, *The Monster Under the Bed* (New York: Simon & Schuster, 1995).

2. David McClelland, *The Achievement Motive* (New York: Irvington Publishers Press, 1976). (Originally published in 1953.)

3. Lawrence J. Peter, *The Peter Principle* (New York: Bantam Books, 1970).

4. Mihaly Csikszentmihalyi, *Flow: The Psychology of Optimal Experience* (New York: HarperCollins, 1991).

5. To test your emotional intelligence, try this Web site: http://www.utne.com/azEQ.tmpl. Accessed January 21, 2001.

6. Daniel Goleman, *Emotional Intelligence* (New York: Bantam, 1995) and *Working with Emotional Intelligence* (New York: Bantam, 1998). For Goleman's bio, see http://www.edge.org/3rd_culture/bios/goleman.html. Accessed October 20, 2000.

7. Daniel Goleman, "Leadership That Gets Results," *Harvard Business Review* (March/April, 2000): 78–90. See http://www.hbsp.harvard.edu/hbsp/prod_detail.asp?R00204 for a downloadable version. Accessed October 20, 2000.

8. The Executive Coaching and Resource Network can be reached on-line at http://www.Executive-Coaching.com/.

9. The Changing Times Web site is at http://www.less-stress.com/index.htm.

10. For a great chapter on stress management, see David Whetten and Kim Cameron, *Developing Management Skills* (Reading, Mass.: Addison-Wesley, 1998). An outline can be found at the following Web site: http://www.loc.gov/catdir/toc/96–226021.html. Accessed October 20, 2000.

11. There are many books and resources on Mind Tools. For a start, see http://www.mindtools.com/page5.html. Accessed October 20, 2000.
12. John H. Kerr, Amanda Griffiths, and Tom Cox, eds., *Workplace Health, Employee Fitness, and Exercise* (London: Taylor & Francis, 1996).
13. On need for achievement, see http://www.accel-team.com/human_relations/hrels_06_mcclelland.html. Accessed January 21, 2001.

Chapter Eight

1. John Haughey, *The Holy Use of Money* (New York: Doubleday, 1986).
2. Barry Posner, "Comparing Recruiter, Student, and Faculty Perceptions," *Personnel Psychology* 34 (1981): 329–337.
3. Christopher Jencks, Lauri Perman, and Lee Rainwater, "What Is a Good Job? A New Indicator of Labor Market Success," *American Journal of Sociology* 93, no. 6 (May 1988): 1322–1357. The data are from a 1980 survey of job characteristics designed by the authors. The telephone survey comprised 809 men and women over the age of eighteen who worked at least twenty hours a week for pay at one job, and no more than ten hours a week for pay at any other job. The average interview took about forty minutes.
4. Note too that these explained 44 percent of the variance in answers to the question, "How does your job compare with the average job, with the AVERAGE job being 100?"
5. Barbara Parus, "Building a Company of Owners," *ACA News* (January, 2000): 33–35.
6. Blake Ashforth and Glenn Kreiner, "How Can You Do It? Dirty Work and the Challenge of Constructing a Positive Identity," *Academy of Management Review* 24, no. 3 (July 1999): 413–434.
7. Scott Adams, *The Dilbert Principle* (New York: HarperCollins, 1996).
8. Bennett J. Tepper, "Consequences of Abusive Supervision," *Academy of Management Journal* 43, no. 2 (2000): 178–190.
9. Amy Zipkin, "The Wisdom of Thoughtfulness," *New York Times* (May 31, 2000): C1.

10. Zipkin, "The Wisdom of Thoughtfulness."
11. Zipkin, "The Wisdom of Thoughtfulness."
12. Lynne Andersson and Christine Pearson, "Tit for Tat? The Spiraling Effect of Incivility in the Workplace," *Academy of Management Review* 24, no. 3 (1999): 452–471.
13. Jill Rosenfeld, "These Lawyers Are Red Hot," *Fast Company* 34 (May 2000): 74.
14. For an extensive discussion, see Frederick Herzberg, Bernard Mausner, and Barbara Bloch Snyderman, *The Motivation to Work* (New Brunswick, N.J.: Transaction, 1993). (First published in 1959.)
15. This list was developed by Crane Brinton in *A History of Western Morals* (New York: Paragon House, 1990).
16. Mark R. Edwards and Ann. J. Ewen, *360-Degree Feedback: The Powerful New Model for Employee Assistance and Performance Improvement* (New York: AMACOM, 1996). See my review of this book in *ACA News* (June 1997): 21.
17. Christena E. Nippert-Eng, *Home and Work: Negotiating Boundaries Through Everyday Life* (Chicago: University of Chicago Press, 1996).
18. Sue Shellenbarger, "What Job Candidates Really Want to Know: Will I Have a Life?" *Wall Street Journal* (November 17, 1999): B1.
19. William Whyte, *The Organization Man* (Garden City, N.Y.: Doubleday, 1956).
20. Juliet Schor, *The Overworked American* (New York: Basic Books, 1991).
21. Arlie Russell Hochschild, *The Second Shift* (New York: Viking, 1989).
22. Arlie Russell Hochschild, *The Time Bind* (New York: Holt, 1997).
23. Weekend Journal, "Give Me a Break!" *Wall Street Journal* (May 5, 2000): W1, W4.
24. Claire Rains, *Beyond Generation X* (Menlo Park, Calif.: Crisp Publications, 1997), back cover.
25. Bob Nelson, *1001 Ways to Reward Employees* (New York: Workman, 1994).
26. The Public Administration Web site (http://www.hrm.napawash.org/Reports/Excerpts/work.htm) is excellent. Accessed October 20, 2000.

Chapter Nine

1. Noel Tichy and Mary Anne Devanna, *The Transformational Leader* (New York: Wiley, 1986).
2. To continue this analogy a bit, the high-end old hotel has hidden costs, amenities that only a few want, and a set of ingrained procedures and expectations that many guests no longer need or wish to meet.
3. The boiled frog metaphor comes from the old science experiment in which you placed a frog in a pan of cool water and slowly heated the water. Incrementally adjusting, the frog did not realize the approaching lethality of temperature, and would, if not removed, boil to death. In business this phenomenon is called the "just noticeable difference syndrome." For many organizations, the change in the environment is slow enough that they do not see it, and so they fail to act. They experience slow death. For other organizations, even if the change is rapid, the insulation of the top team means that what they see is "same old same old." They experience fast death.
4. Rosabeth Moss Kanter, *The Change Masters* (New York: Simon & Schuster, 1983), pp. 221–225.
5. Kanter, *The Change Masters,* p. 223.
6. Herbert Simon, Donald Smithberg, and Victor Thompson, *Public Administration* (New York: Knopf, 1950).
7. "Welcome to WorldatWork," *Workspan* (June 2000): 3. *(Workspan,* the magazine of WorldatWork, was formerly *American Compensation Association News.)*

Appendix

1. Howard Risher, "Are Public Employers Ready for a 'New Pay' Program?" *Public Personnel Management* 28, no. 3 (Fall 1999): 323–343.
2. Paul Clolery, "NPT Salary Survey." Available on-line at http://www.nptimes.com/Feb00/00salaries.html.

The Author

John E. Tropman received his B.A. in sociology and government from Oberlin College, his master's degree from the University of Chicago, and his Ph.D. in sociology from the University of Michigan. He has spent his career at the University of Michigan, teaching nonprofit management courses at the School of Social Work, organizational behavior and human resources management courses at the Business School, and effective decision making and creativity in the executive education program. In addition, he has taught leadership and other material at the executive education program at Carnegie Mellon University in Pittsburgh.

Tropman has written and edited many books; his recent works include *Enhancing Physician Performance* (edited with Scott B. Ransom and William W. Pinsky), *Making Meetings Work, Management of Ideas in the Creating Organization, Does America Hate the Poor?* and *Nonprofit Boards: What to Do and How to Do It* (with Elmer J. Tropman).

Through his consultancy, High Quality Decisions, Tropman presents programs on effective meetings and team decision making throughout the country. He has worked with human service organizations such as the United Way of America, the Jewish

Federation of Metro Detroit, and Lutheran Social Services of Michigan, as well as with other nonprofits. He has also worked with companies such as Abbott Labs, DuPont, General Motors (Cadillac), and Ford, as well as governmental organizations such as the General Accounting Office and the Air Force.

Tropman is married and has three children and two grand-children.

Index